The School Mission Statement

Values, Goals, and Identities in American Education

Steven E. Stemler, Ph.D.
Damian J. Bebell, Ph.D.

Eye On Education
6 Depot Way West, Suite 106
Larchmont, NY 10538
(914) 833–0551
(914) 833–0761 fax
www.eyeoneducation.com

Library of Congress Cataloging-in-Publication Data

Stemler, Steven E.
The school mission statement : values, goals, and identities in American
education/Steven E. Stemler, Damian J. Bebell.
        p.   cm.
Includes bibliographical references.
ISBN 978-1-59667-214-7
1. Education—Aims and objectives—United States.
2. Educational planning—United States.
3. Education—Philosophy.
4. Mission statements—United States.
I. Bebell, Damian J.
II. Title.
LA210.S716 2012
370.973—dc23   2011048060

Sponsoring Editor: Robert Sickles
Production Editor: Lauren Beebe
Copyeditor: Dorothy D. Anderson
Designer and Compositor: Matthew Williams, click! Publishing Services
Cover Designer: Dave Strauss, 3FoldDesign

Also Available from EYE ON EDUCATION

Lead On!
Motivational Lessons for School Leaders
Pete Hall

The Principal's Guide to the First 100 Days of the School Year:
Creating Instructional Momentum
Shawn Joseph

What Great Principals Do Differently:
Eighteen Things That Matter Most
(Second Edition)
Todd Whitaker

Rigor in Your School:
A Toolkit for Leaders
Ronald Williamson & Barbara R. Blackburn

Professional Development: What Works
(Second Edition)
Sally J. Zepeda

Building School Culture One Week at a Time
Jeffrey Zoul

Leading School Change:
9 Strategies to Bring Everybody on Board
Todd Whitaker

School-Community Relations
(Third Edition)
Douglas J. Fiore

Introduction to Educational Administration:
Standards, Theory, and Practice
(Second Edition)
Douglas J. Fiore

Examining What We Do to Improve Our Schools:
8 Steps from Analysis to Action
Sandra Harris, Stacey Edmonson, & Julie Combs

Contents

About the Authors ix
Acknowledgements ix
Introduction: What Is the Purpose of School? xi

Part I: Background on the Purpose of School and School Mission Statements 1
  1 Diverse Perspectives on the Purpose of School 3
    Academic Perspectives 3
    Legislative Perspectives 4
    Legal Perspectives 6
    Business Perspectives 7
    Summary 8

  2 The Value of School Mission Statements 9
    Mission Statements and School Accrediting 10
    Mission Statements and School Effectiveness 11
    Mission Statements Can Be Quantitatively Summarized 12
    Past Research on Public School Mission Statements in America 13
    A Word About What Follows 16
    Some Technical Notes 16

Part II: School Mission Statements 19
  3 Public Elementary Schools 21
  4 Public Middle Schools 30
  5 Public High Schools 42
  6 Vocational/Career/Technical Education Schools 53
  7 Magnet Schools 64
  8 Charter Schools 74
  9 Native American/Tribal Schools 84
 10 Parochial Schools 91
 11 Waldorf Schools 102
 12 Montessori Schools 111
 13 Apple Computer Schools of Distinction 119
 14 Award Winning Schools 129

Part III: Analysis and Conclusions 151

15 Common and Unique Elements to School Mission Statements 153
   Analysis by School Type. 154
      Public Elementary Schools 154
      Public Middle Schools 155
      Public High Schools 157
      Vocational/Career/Technical Education Schools 158
      Magnet Schools 159
      Charter Schools 160
      Native American/Tribal Schools 162
      Parochial Schools 163
      Waldorf Schools. 165
      Montessori Schools 167
      Apple Schools of Distinction. 168
      Award Winning Schools. 169
   Conclusion 170

16 Crafting Your Own School Mission Statement 174
   Emotional Development. 175
      Specific Character Traits. 175
      Love of Learning. 176
      Moral and Ethical Development. 177
      Existential Values 178
      Environment Elements. 179
   Cognitive Development 182
      Knowledge and Skills. 182
      Academic Attitude 183
      Academic Achievement 184
      Academic Curriculum 185
   Challenging Environment 188
      Expectations of Students 188
      Instructional Elements 189
      Environmental Elements 191
   Safe/Nurturing Environment 193
      Safe Environment 193
      Nurturing Environment. 194
      Specific Components of a Nurturing Environment. 195
   Civic Development 197
      Responsible Citizens. 197
      Productive Citizens. 198

Leadership 199
Service and Responsibility. 199
Integration Into Local Community. 201
Students Contributing to Community. 201
Community Working Together. 202
Community Focused on Developing Responsible Students 203
Integration Into Global Community. 205
Adapt to a Changing World 205
Develop Global Leaders. 205
Prepare Globally Responsible Citizens 206
Prepare for Global Competition 207
Social Development. 208
Social Skills. 209
Social Attitudes 210
Vocational Preparation 211
Vocational Skills 211
Focus on Job Preparation. 212
Response to External Indicators 213
Spiritual Development 214
Development of Specific Values 215
Holistic Emphasis 215
Physical Development 217

Conclusion 219

Index of Schools by Grade Level. 221
Index of Schools by Urbanicity 227
Index of Schools by Percent Free Lunch. 231

References. 235

About the Authors

Steven E. Stemler is an Assistant Professor of Psychology at Wesleyan University and is the current President of the New England Educational Research Organization (NEERO). He received his doctorate in Educational Research, Measurement, and Evaluation from Boston College, where he worked at the Center for the Study of Testing, Evaluation, and Educational Policy and the TIMSS International Study Center. Prior to joining the faculty at Wesleyan, Steve spent four years at Yale University, where he was an Associate Research Scientist in the Department of Psychology. His area of expertise is testing and assessment, with a special emphasis on the domains of social, emotional, and practical intelligence; creativity; intercultural literacy; and ethical reasoning.

Damian Bebell is an Assistant Research Professor at Boston College's Lynch School of Education and a Senior Research Associate at the Center for the Study of Testing, Evaluation, and Educational Policy. Currently, Damian is directing multiple evaluation studies investigating the effects of 1-to-1 technology programs on teaching and learning, including collaborative research with the Boston Public Schools and the New York City Public Schools. Damian's research interests include the development and refinement of educational tools and methods, education reform, testing, and the impacts of educational technology on teaching and learning.

Acknowledgements
We would like to gratefully acknowledge the support of our friends and colleagues at Wesleyan University and Boston College, especially Rebecca Lange, Melanie Ferdinand, and Dan McNeish at Wesleyan for their assistance in preparing this book. In addition, we would like to thank Bob Sickles and Lauren Beebe at Eye On Education for their encouragement, valuable suggestions, and patience.

Introduction

What Is the Purpose of School?

As someone interested in education, you have probably found yourself reflecting on this important question at some point in your career. Although the question itself appears simple and straightforward, the answer is often deceptively complex. Philosophers, scientists, politicians, government organizations, private corporations, and the general public have all questioned and examined the purposes of school from their own perspectives. Over the past decade, we have systematically explored this question across a series of research studies, and we have found much common ground among different constituents. What is especially intriguing, however, and what has led us to this book, is the tremendous diversity we have discovered across American schools in describing their own perspectives and purposes through their school mission statements. Even in today's era of school consolidation and state and national standardization, American schools primarily continue to serve the needs of their individual local communities and remain locally controlled and operated, a point that our work with school mission statements makes abundantly clear.

One of the most fundamental and important tasks for educational leaders is to clearly articulate the purpose of schooling guiding their local educational community. We hope that by examining and reflecting on a purposefully diverse sample of American school mission statements, this book may help readers clarify their own values and perspectives on the purpose of schooling.

This book is divided into three parts. In Part I, we provide the reader with relevant background and context. Specifically, Chapter 1 contains a brief historical summary of the purposes of school as articulated by different stakeholders over time. In Chapter 2, we describe the scientific research we have conducted that has allowed for the systematic and quantitative analysis of school mission statements. We present a summary of our methodological approach and the interesting findings from this research. The reader may find our framework useful for interpreting the mission statements provided in the subsequent chapters of this book.

In Part II of the book, we present the actual mission statements and school characteristics for a subsample of 111 distinctive schools of different varieties. Chapters 3 through 14 include mission statements from public elementary schools, public middle schools, public high schools, vocational schools, magnet schools, charter schools, Native American schools, parochial schools, Waldorf schools, Montessori schools, schools recognized as Apple Computer Schools of Distinction, and award winning schools. In each chapter, we first provide the reader with some historical background on the type of school that is the focus of the chapter and then describe the prevalence and role of each school type in the American K–12 education landscape. Each chapter then contains a sample of school mission statements collected in 2011, as well as information on the school's location, size, and student population. These schools illustrate the broad range of missions that currently exist across the American educational landscape as well as some of the best and most innovative educational programs in the country.

Finally, Part III serves as an opportunity for reflection. In Chapter 15, we describe some of the key similarities and differences we have observed across the sample of school mission statements included in this book. Chapter 16 is designed to help facilitate the process of creating a mission statement. We describe how educators can use the information in this book to assist them in the process of developing and revising their schools' mission statements.

PART I

Background on the Purpose of School and School Mission Statements

1

Diverse Perspectives on the Purpose of School

At present, opinion is divided about the subjects of education. People do not take the same view about what should be learned by the young, either with a view to human excellence or a view to the best possible life, nor is it clear whether education should be directed mainly to the intellect or to moral character . . . [,] whether the proper studies to be pursued are those that are useful in life, or those that make for excellence, or those that advance the bounds of knowledge. . . . Men do not all honor the same distinctive human excellence and so naturally they differ about the proper training for it.

—Aristotle as quoted in Knight, 1989

A wide variety of educational stakeholders have questioned and considered the purposes of schooling for hundreds, even thousands, of years. Thus, before proceeding with our examination of modern American school mission statements, we believe it is useful to consider the perspectives on school purpose found in different arenas, including the academic, legislative, legal, and business communities.

Academic Perspectives

Educational philosophers were among the first group of individuals to write about and formally debate the different purposes of schools. Ancient philosophers as diverse as Aristotle, Plato, Mo Tzu, and Confucius wrote extensively on the purpose and role of education and schooling in their respective cultures (Noddings, 1995; Reed & Johnson, 1996). These great thinkers shared some common ideas about what schools should exist to do, but each of them also had their own unique perspectives on the role of schooling within a given culture and civilization.

In more modern times, American educational philosophers such as John Dewey, George Counts, and Mortimore Adler have each proposed systematic and detailed arguments regarding the purpose of schooling in American society. For example, Dewey (1938) argued that the primary purpose of education and schooling is not so much to prepare students to live a useful life, but to teach them how to live pragmatically and immediately in their current environment. By contrast, Counts, a leading progressive educator in the 1930s, critiqued Dewey's philosophy, stating, "the weakness of progressive education thus lies in the fact that it has elaborated no theory of social welfare, unless it be that of anarchy or extreme individualism" (1978, p. 5). To Counts, the purpose of school was less about preparing individuals to live independently and more about preparing individuals to live as members of a society. Indeed, the role of schooling, according to Counts, was to equip individuals with the skills necessary to participate in the social life of their community and to change the nature of the social order as needed or desired. In 1982, the notable educator and philosopher Mortimer Adler wrote *The Paideia Proposal*, which integrated the ideas of Dewey and Counts, as well as his own. Specifically, Adler suggested that there are three objectives of children's schooling: (1) the development of citizenship, (2) personal growth or self-improvement, and (3) occupational preparation.

The great historian of education David Tyack (1988) has argued that from a historical perspective, the purpose of schooling has been tied to social and economic needs. More recently, some sociologists have argued that schools exist primarily to serve a practical credentialing function in society (Labaree, 1997). Expanding on the pragmatic purpose of school, deMarrais and LeCompte (1995) outlined four major purposes of schooling, which include (1) intellectual purposes such as the development of mathematical and reading skills, (2) political purposes such as the assimilation of immigrants, (3) economic purposes such as job preparation, and (4) social purposes such as the development of social and moral responsibility.

Legislative Perspectives

While the perspective of educational philosophers provides us with an important backdrop against which to consider the question of school purpose, a more pragmatic perspective can be ascertained from local, state, and federal governments. Because the United States Constitution makes no mention of the purpose or function of schools, the responsibility for schooling and formal education is a matter delegated to each state. State constitutions vary in the degree to which they explicate the purposes of schooling, but perhaps the most comprehensive view is put forth by the Massachusetts constitution. Massachusetts provides a particularly interesting example because it was the first state constitution written in the US, and it was authored by John Adams, the second president of the United States. Adams wrote pointedly and directly to the purpose and role of schooling in post-colonial Massachusetts:

> Wisdom, and knowledge, as well as virtue, diffused generally among the body of the people, being necessary for the preservation of their rights and liberties; and as these depend on spreading the opportunities and advantages of education in the various parts of the country, and among the different orders of the people, it shall be the duty of legislatures and magistrates, in all future periods of this commonwealth, to cherish the interests of literature and the sciences, and all seminaries of them; especially the university at Cambridge, public schools and grammar schools in the towns; to encourage private societies and public institutions, rewards and immunities, for the promotion of agriculture, arts, sciences, commerce, trades, manufactures, and a natural history of the country; to countenance and inculcate the principles of humanity and general benevolence, public and private charity, industry and frugality, honesty and punctuality in their dealings; sincerity, good humor, and all social affections, and generous sentiments among the people. (187th General Court of the Commonwealth of Massachusetts, 2010)

Thus, as early as 1780, the Massachusetts constitution formally established a broad, multifaceted scope for education. Since that time, individual states have developed educational aspirations that reflect the needs of their residents. For example, the state constitution of Florida articulates both common and unique elements related to the purpose of school compared to Massachusetts. Specifically, the Florida constitution, rewritten in 2006, clearly illustrates Florida's concern with providing a safe environment for its children. In addition, the constitution emphasizes early childhood development and the importance of cognitive, social, and emotional development:

> The education of children is a fundamental value of the people of the State of Florida. It is, therefore, a paramount duty of the state to make adequate provision for the education of all children residing within its borders. Adequate provision shall be made by law for a

uniform, efficient, safe, secure, and high quality system of free public schools that allows students to obtain a high quality education and for the establishment, maintenance, and operation of institutions of higher learning and other public education programs that the needs of the people may require. . . . (b) Every four-year old child in Florida shall be provided by the State a high quality pre-kindergarten learning opportunity in the form of an early childhood development and education program which shall be voluntary, high quality, free, and delivered according to professionally accepted standards. An early childhood development and education program means an organized program designed to address and enhance each child's ability to make age appropriate progress in an appropriate range of settings in the development of language and cognitive capabilities and emotional, social, regulatory and moral capacities through education in basic skills and such other skills as the Legislature may determine to be appropriate. (Florida Legislature, 2010)

Legal Perspectives

An additional source of opinion on the purposes of American schooling has come from the judicial branch. Specifically, in the late 1980s, a series of landmark legal cases helped redefine the purposes and responsibilities of US schools. In 1989, the Kentucky State Supreme Court ordered the general assembly to provide funding "sufficient to provide each child in Kentucky an adequate education" and to reform the property tax system (*Rose v. Council for Better Education*, 1989). In defining what constitutes an adequate public education, the court enumerated seven learning goals that have been widely cited as precedent and since adopted by numerous other states, including Massachusetts (e.g., *McDuffy v. Secretary*, 1993). The seven distinct components of education include the development of the following:

(i) sufficient oral and written communication skills to enable a student to function in a complex and readily changing civilization;

(ii) sufficient knowledge of economic, social, and political systems to enable students to make informed choices;

(iii) sufficient understanding of government processes to enable the student to understand the issues that affect his or her community, state, and nation;

(iv) sufficient self-knowledge and knowledge of his or her mental and physical wellness;

(v)   sufficient grounding in the arts to enable each student to appreciate his or her cultural and historical heritage;

(vi) sufficient training or preparation for advanced training in either academic or vocational fields so as to enable each child to choose and pursue life work intelligently; and

(vii) sufficient level of academic or vocational skills to enable public school students to compete favorably with their counterparts in surrounding states, in academics or in the job market. (McDuffy v. Secretary, 1993)

In recognizing the many goals of American public education, the supreme courts of Kentucky and many other states have echoed the sentiment that public schooling is not intended to be an exclusively academic or cognitive experience for students. Indeed, the Kentucky and Massachusetts decisions make it clear that cognitive outcomes are only one among many aims of schooling. There is no language in these decisions that implies cognitive skills should receive the primary emphasis over and above civic, emotional, and vocational purposes.

Business Perspectives

Another research-based approach to understanding the purpose of school has come from researchers using survey and interview methodologies. Specifically, survey methods have been used to illustrate different stakeholders' perspectives concerning the purpose of American schools. For example, a survey of California residents (Immerwahl, 2000) showed that the majority of the respondents believed that the California higher education system indeed served a wide range of educational objectives. The poll showed that the majority of California tax payers felt the purpose of post-secondary education was to develop a sense of maturity and an ability to manage independently (71 percent), develop skills to get along with people different from oneself (68 percent), develop problem-solving and thinking abilities (63 percent), develop specific expertise and knowledge in a chosen career (60 percent), develop writing and speaking ability (57 percent), and develop a sense of responsible citizenship (44 percent).

Similarly, a 2005 survey study examined the purpose of post-secondary school from the perspective of employers and business leaders. The John J. Heldrich Center for Workforce Development (2005) asked more than 400 New Jersey employers to express their views on the purpose of higher education and to evaluate how well the state's colleges and universities were preparing students across sixteen skill areas. The results revealed that employers cited teamwork (46 percent of respondents), social skills and critical thinking (32 percent, respectively), and integrity and honesty (30 percent) as the most important qualities they expected educated students to possess.

An evaluation of past issues of *Recruiting Trends* (Gardner, 2007), a publication based on information supplied by hundreds of companies and organizations concerning the recruitment of recent college graduates, revealed what skills employers were specifically seeking in their recruits. An analysis of the publication indicates the most recent trends of recruitment that are taking hold in the workforce. In 2002 to 2003, ethics and integrity were considered the most important competencies. The following year, employers expressed their preference for college students to have better developed skills in communication, personal attributes (work ethic, flexibility, initiative, and motivation), teamwork, interpersonal skills, and learning (willing to learn continuously new skills and ideas). Finally, the 2005 to 2006 issue observes that an emerging skill is geographic awareness and a global understanding of events as they pertain to the company and industrial sector.

Summary

As this brief summary of philosophical and political perspectives illustrates, there *has been* substantial thought and debate about the purposes of schooling in American culture. From our review, it is clear that both theorists and policy makers recognize that there are multiple purposes for schooling in American society today. However, despite generations of advances in social science research, the amount of systematic empirical research examining broader questions of school purpose remains strikingly limited. In addition, despite the current educational emphasis on reflection and measurement, remarkably little attention paid has been paid to the school's perspective on its actual role and purpose. Who is asking the big questions?

Recognizing the utility of empirical methodologies and the lack of data and resources representing the schools' own perspectives, we have conducted a series of empirical studies to categorize and quantify the purpose of school from the perspective of today's schools themselves. Our research in this area is described in the next chapter.

2

The Value of School Mission Statements

The early years of the 21st century have seen an increased emphasis on data-driven decision making, evidence-based interventions, and outcomes-based education (as indicated by student test score results). Each of these policy approaches depends on precise, quantifiable information based on empirical (observable) data. Curiously, however, despite the long tradition of commentary on the topic of school purpose, hardly any of the debate and discourse regarding this fundamental and big picture topic in education seems rooted in empirical research.

Many reasonable and well-informed individuals hold vastly different opinions on some of the most important educational issues of the day (e.g., high-stakes testing, differentiated instruction, educational computing, etc.). Upon reflection, these differences of opinion can often be traced back to different perspectives on the fundamental purposes of school. Indeed, given the detail with which educators and researchers have applied quantitative methodologies to minuscule components of various educational strategies and reform models, we have been somewhat astonished to discover the scant empirical educational research focused on the big picture educational issues.

To date, only a few examples of research-based investigations and approaches have focused on school purpose. As one example, Tanner and Tanner (1990) applied document analysis to historic textbooks and teacher lesson plans to demonstrate shifts in the role and purpose of American education over the past two centuries. For example, they found that in the 1830s, the inculcation of morality and character development was frequently the dominant purpose of American schools. By the 1880s, however, the primary emphasis had shifted toward cognitive and academic development. The prime objective of education in that era was to prepare the next generation of thinkers while serving to "weed out those unable to profit from a curriculum aimed at developing intellectual power" (Tanner & Tanner, 1990, p. 106).

The other major research-based approach has involved survey research methods (John J. Heldrich Center for Workforce Development, 2005; Immerwahl, 2000). However, there has remained a notable absence of research examining the question of purpose from the perspective of the schools and their constituents. We hypothesized that this omission could be attributable to the lack of any clearly accepted methodological approach for ascertaining the school perspective. In the late 1990s, we began to examine the first generation of school websites where one of the first items that schools tended to post were their mission statements. Looking at the ease of access as well as their central role, we identified school mission statements as a worthwhile and largely untapped resource for our inquiry. After a decade of research involving many different studies of school mission statements (Stemler & Bebell, 1999; Bebell & Stemler, 2004; Stemler, Bebell, & Sonnabend, 2011), we are convinced that a school's own mission statement provides an accessible and meaningful window for further exploration of the purpose of school.

Before we turn this book over to examples of actual school mission statements we have collected from American schools, we first summarize our rationale for choosing school mission statements as a source of empirical research data. We then briefly outline our approach for coding and quantifying the different topics and various ideas present in school mission statements.

Mission Statements and School Accrediting

School mission statements serve many important roles for schools. First, nearly all major school accrediting bodies recognize and require a mission statement from schools seeking accreditation (AdvancED, 2010). Indeed, the very first standard articulated by the nation's largest secondary school accreditation body requires that

> The school establishes and communicates a shared purpose and direction for improving the performance of students and the effectiveness of the school. In fulfillment of the standard, the school: (i) establishes a vision for the school in collaboration with its key stakeholders, (ii) communicates the vision and purpose to build stakeholder understanding and support, (iii) identifies goals to advance the vision, (iv) ensures that the school's vision and purpose guide the learning process, and (v) reviews its vision and purpose systematically and revises them when appropriate. (AdvancED, 2010, p. 1)

As articulated by most accrediting boards (as well as many business, civic, and private organizations in America), mission statements represent an important summation or distillation of an organization's core goals represented by concise and simple statements that communicate broad themes (Abrahams, 2007, 1995; Emil, 2001). Furthermore, school mission statements are one of the only written documents outlining the purpose that nearly all schools have. The fact that nearly all American schools have a mission statement thus provides a common measure allowing for systematic comparison even across diverse institutions.

Mission Statements and School Effectiveness

A number of research inquiries in the area of school effectiveness have consistently shown that commitment to a shared mission is one of the leading factors differentiating more effective schools from less effective schools (Claus & Chamaine, 1985; Druian & Butler 1987; Perkins, 1992; Renchler, 1991; Renihan, Renihan, & Waldron 1986; Rutter & Maughan, 2002; Teddlie & Reynolds, 2000). Researchers suggest that the school mission statement can serve to represent the core philosophy and working ethos of a school and that a shared mission may be a necessary prerequisite for an effective and highly functioning school. Although we would not argue that the mission is the only indicator of a school's cultural values, we do argue that it provides a straightforward and accessible indicator.

As part of our prior research, we conducted an interview study with a sample of American public school principals to learn more about how different schools create, maintain, and use their mission statements (Stemler, Bebell, & Sonnabend, 2011). The majority of school leaders told us that the creation of their school mission statements had been a collaborative process involving many authors within the school community. Although the content of a school mission statement may consider global and national objectives, these leaders made it clear that the mission itself is most often a direct product of the immediate school community (students, teachers, administrators, parents, and members of the local community). Similarly, the principals in our study reported that staff often had high levels of familiarity with the school mission.

Principals noted that high school mission statements tend to be revised frequently, suggesting that school missions can be dynamic and malleable. For the principals themselves, mission statements were widely cited as an important tool for shaping school vision and practice. Such results echo the school effectiveness literature, which has found that schools typically identified as more effective tend to have a stronger commitment to a shared vision. Finally, in direct response to a question on whether school mission statements reflect actual school practices and core goals, principals overwhelmingly felt that their own school mission statements reflected the actual practices and aims present in their school.

Mission Statements Can Be Quantitatively Summarized

Over the past decade, emerging research has demonstrated that mission statements can be systematically and reliably coded by applying content analysis techniques (Bebell & Stemler, 2004; Berleur & Harvanek, 1997; Stemler, 2001; Stemler & Bebell, 1999; Stober, 1997). In 1999, we developed a coding rubric for school mission statements that allowed such statements to be classified according to eleven broad themes. These mission statement themes include the following:

1. foster cognitive development
2. foster social development
3. foster emotional development
4. foster civic development
5. foster physical development
6. foster vocational preparation
7. integrate into local community
8. integrate into global community
9. foster spiritual development
10. provide safe/nurturing environment, and
11. provide challenging environment

Generally, the first nine of these categories may be thought of in terms of educational "outputs," or things schools try to develop in students. The final two themes may be more appropriately categorized as educational "inputs," or things schools focus on developing as part of the school climate or environment. An example of how the scoring rubric is applied is shown in Figure 2.1.

Thus, any school mission statement can be coded on eleven independent traits. Once school mission statements have been coded, it is possible to conduct statistical analyses of these traits across samples of schools. Across a series of studies over the past decade, we found our rating system to be both easy to use and highly reliable (Bebell & Stemler, 2004; Stemler & Bebell, 1999; Stemler, Bebell, & Sonnabend, 2011).

FIGURE 2.1 Scoring Rubric

EXAMPLE A

School mission statement that incorporates many different themes:

"In *partnership with students, parents and community*,[7] Rutland High School offers diverse learning opportunities and strives to meet the *academic*,[1] *social*,[2] *physical*[5] and *emotional*[3] needs of all its students. We provide a *safe, orderly, healthy environment*[10] that is conducive to teaching and learning and a school climate that values mutual respect and dignity. Rutland High School graduates will possess the *skills and knowledge*[1] necessary to be *lifelong learners*[3] and *productive citizens*.[4]" (Rutland Senior High School—Rutland, Vermont)

Coding:
[1]cognitive development, [2]social development, [3]emotional development, [4]civic development, [5]physical development, [7]local community, [10]safe environment

---

EXAMPLE B

Phrases used in school mission statements with no codable themes:

- "Striving for excellence"
- "Building tomorrow's leaders today"

Past Research on Public School Mission Statements in America

In one of our most recent studies of school mission statements, we took a random sample of 421 public high schools from ten geographically and politically diverse states and analyzed their mission statements (Stemler, Bebell, & Sonnabend, 2011). We found that like the philosophers and statesmen of history, American schools typically put forward multiple purposes in their school mission statement. In other words, the initial answer to the question of the purpose of school is this: *there are typically many purposes of school.*

Figure 2.2 (page 14) shows the range of different themes present in school mission statements. The number of different themes in each mission statement ranged from 0 to 9, with an average of 3.5. Most American public high schools in our study had at least three or four distinct themes in their mission statements, although occasionally some had many more. Although quite simple, this finding suggests only a very small subset of schools had either vacuous or catch-all mission statements. Instead, the vast majority of the high school statements in our sample focused on a limited and purposive number of themes and objectives.

FIGURE 2.2 Distribution of the Number of Themes Found
Across 421 High School Mission Statements

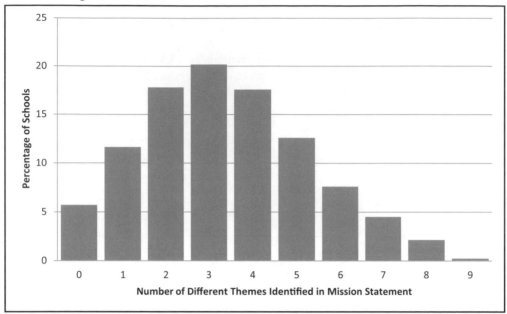

The coding rubric we have presented makes it easy to examine the frequency with which different themes are mentioned across school mission statements and to get some indication as to the dominant school purpose expressed across schools. Figure 2.3 shows the frequency of the eleven mission statement themes across the sample of 421 public schools from our large-scale, randomized sample of American public high schools.

Across this random sample of American public schools, civic development was the most frequently articulated theme (found in 58 percent of school mission statements), followed by emotional development (55 percent) and cognitive development (53 percent). The least frequently cited elements were physical development (8 percent) and spiritual development (1 percent of public schools).

At the broadest level of analysis, high school mission statements showed consensus on at least three major purposes of education across high schools: (1) civic development, (2) emotional development, and (3) cognitive development. Finding three core themes shared across the majority of school mission statements suggests that America's high schools share several common goals and that school purpose may be reasonably standardized. In addition, these three themes shared across the mission statements more or less reflect the same themes and "purposes" represented most commonly by

FIGURE 2.3 Percentage of Schools Endorsing Each Major Theme

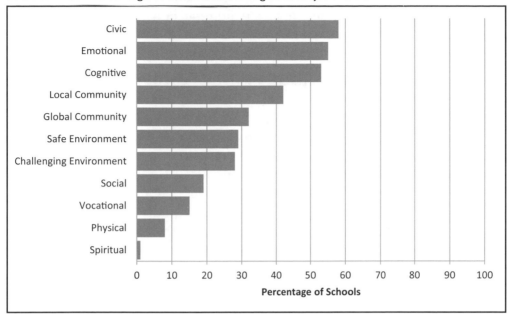

nonschool stakeholders (government leaders, philosophers, parents, business leaders, etc.).

Viewed from another perspective, however, one might point out that only these three themes (civic, emotional, and cognitive development) were found in over 50 percent of the high schools in our study. In other words, many high school mission statements have shared content and themes, but the individual school statements were actually more different than they were alike. Such variance in the results suggest that, at least in many instances, public high schools continue to articulate their overall purpose in terms of individual (local and community) needs, despite the increasing presence of federally and state-mandated educational reforms.

When analyzed by context, interesting differences across the state samples also emerged based across the ten states in the study. For example, in New York and California, both states with historically large immigrant populations, the most dominant theme emphasized was civic development (72 percent of schools in both states). More than a decade after the Columbine High School massacre, Colorado high schools exhibited the largest percentage of mission statements with references to safe learning environments (62 percent). Texas and Florida, the two states recognized as early advocates of standards-based reform, both emphasized the cognitive development theme in their mission statements more frequently than other states in the sample

(64 percent and 65 percent, respectively). Thus, the thematic content of school mission statements does appear to be a valid reflection of local policy.

A Word About What Follows

The remainder of this book is devoted to presenting a purposeful selection of school mission statements from a diverse array of schools and institutional categories. Our aim is to provide educators with a variety of perspectives and examples of K–12 school mission statements illustrating the tremendous range in emphasis that can be found across schools in the United States. Through numerous examples (in Chapters 3 through 14), we hope readers will develop an understanding of the diverse themes and ideas related to school purpose communicated through school mission statements. This understanding is particularly valuable in any community engaged in creating or revising its own school's mission statement. It can also help foster a deeper understanding of the various competing themes and goals American schools currently aim to serve.

The reader does not need to adopt our coding model as a lens to interpret school mission statements, but our goal in providing the rubric is to give readers an additional tool in articulating common themes and trends. In our experience reviewing mission statements from widely differing sectors of the educational community, we have found this rubric to be a useful lens through which to interpret meaningful differences between schools in the themes emphasized in their mission statements. However, we also recognize the limitation of our analytic approach to something as complex as the purpose of school and as linguistically rich as school mission statements, and we encourage others to pursue new and alternative methods to best suit their needs.

Some Technical Notes

All school mission statements and demographic data were collected between February 1, 2011, and October 31, 2011. Schools were selected for participation by a multistep process. Lists of schools of each type were identified from major organizations (e.g., the US Department of Education Blue Ribbon School program). The researchers then randomly selected subsets of schools and also purposefully selected some schools whose mission statements were distinctive. A letter was then sent to each school leader asking for permission to reprint the school's mission statement in the context of this book. We are extremely appreciative to the school leaders of the schools included in this book for allowing us to reproduce their schools' mission statements here. Each school mission statement is reprinted verbatim from the school's website or from the correspondence we received from the school's leadership.

The demographic data gathered for the schools was drawn from the United States Department of Education's National Center for Educational Statistic's Common Core of Data (http://nces.ed.gov/ccd/). We followed the NCES designations to summarize each school's locale (City, Suburb, Town, or Rural), including the subcategories within each of these classifications (see http://nces.ed.gov/ccd/rural_locales.asp for details). Students' ethnicity data were largely gathered from the Common Core of Data.[1] In cases where the data were not available on the CCD website, we searched for the information at www.greatschools.org/.

[1]Student ethnicity data in this book were accurate at the time of publication in 2012. Any discrepancies in student population and ethnicity numbers are due to changing CCD reports.

PART II

School Mission Statements

3

Public Elementary Schools

Although wide ranging, elementary (or primary) schools can be defined as schools that provide students their first compulsory school experience in the United States. Most of the nearly 70,000 US public elementary schools include kindergarten through fifth grade (serving children between five and eleven years of age). Elementary schools serving older students in grades six, seven, and eight were more common before the rise of middle schools beginning in the early 1970s but still thrive in numerous communities. In the majority of elementary schools, students remain in self-contained classrooms with one teacher for the core curriculum subjects, which typically include English language arts, math, science, and social studies/geography, and attend less frequent classes, such as physical education, art, music, and foreign languages, with specialist teachers.

Since 1918, elementary schools have been compulsory across all US states. The required age for children to be enrolled in school ranges by state from five years old (Arkansas, Connecticut, Delaware, Maryland, New Mexico, Oklahoma, South Carolina and Virginia) to eight years old (Pennsylvania and Washington). The determination of which school a student attends is typically driven by geographical regulations. Typically, students must be residents of the city or town where the school is located; however, exemptions are possible. The residency issue is especially pertinent as public elementary schools are publicly funded by local property taxes. The mission statements shared in this chapter represent elementary schools from across the country. As the accompanying demographic statistics show, these schools serve a wide range of different communities and students.

Source: US Department of Education, National Center for Education Statistics (2011).

DeSoto Central Elementary School
Southaven, Mississippi

Mission Statement

The mission of DeSoto Central Elementary School is to create a safe, positive environment in which students can experience optimal learning and develop moral character which will enable them to become productive citizens in a multi-cultural, changing society.

School Characteristics:

Grade Levels: PreK–5
Locale: Rural-fringe
Total Students: 1,370
Male-Female Ratio: 53:47
Student-Teacher Ratio: 20.8:1
Free Lunch Eligible: 16.6%
Reduced-Price Lunch Eligible: 7.2%

Ethnicity	N	%
AmerInd/Alaskan	0	0.0
Asian	60	4.4
Black	244	17.8
Hispanic	31	2.3
White	1,035	75.5

General Information:

2411 Central Parkway
Southaven, MS 38672
(662) 349-6234
www.desotocountyschools.org/subsite/dce

Doña Ana Elementary School
Las Cruces, New Mexico

Mission Statement

Our goal at Doña Ana Elementary is to nurture and empower every student to reach their full potential, giving them many opportunities to adapt to their changing world and instill a love of learning.

School Characteristics:

Grade Levels: PreK–5
Locale: Suburb-midsize
Total Students: 424
Male-Female Ratio: 49:51
Student-Teacher Ratio: 13.2:1
Free Lunch Eligible: 65.3%
Reduced-Price Lunch Eligible: 10.1%

Ethnicity	N	%
AmerInd/Alaskan	1	0.2
Asian	0	0.0
Black	8	1.9
Hispanic	354	83.5
White	61	14.4

General Information:

5551 Camino de Flores
Las Cruces, NM 88001
(505) 527-5800
http://donaana.lcps.k12.nm.us/index.shtml

Holiday Elementary School
Hopkinsville, Kentucky

Mission Statement

The Holiday Elementary School staff believes it is our responsibility to help all children learn today to achieve a brighter tomorrow.

School Characteristics:

Grade Levels: PreK–5
Locale: Town-distant
Total Students: 598
Male-Female Ratio: 50:50
Student-Teacher Ratio: 19.3:1
Free Lunch Eligible: 47.1%
Reduced-Price Lunch Eligible: 13.2%

Ethnicity	N	%
AmerInd/Alaskan	0	0.0
Asian	16	2.8
Black	165	28.9
Hispanic	17	3.0
White	372	65.3

General Information:

3910 Nassau Circle
Hopkinsville, KY 42240
(270) 887-7210
www.christian.k12.ky.us/HolidayElementary.cfm?subpage=592360

Jerome W. Stamply Elementary School
Clarksdale, Mississippi

Mission Statement

Our mission is to provide the highest quality of education for our children by broadening their minds and laying the foundation for life-long learning.

School Characteristics:

Grade Levels: K–5
Locale: Town-remote
Total Students: 268
Male-Female Ratio: 48:52
Student-Teacher Ratio: 17.6:1
Free Lunch Eligible: 95.1%
Reduced-Price Lunch Eligible: 1.9%

Ethnicity	N	%
AmerInd/Alaskan	0	0.0
Asian	1	0.4
Black	266	99.3
Hispanic	0	0.0
White	0	0.0
Two or more races	1	0.4

General Information:

P.O. Box 1088
Clarksdale, MS 38614
(662) 627-8570
www.cmsd.k12.ms.us/stampley/default.htm

Lincoln Elementary School
Gallup, New Mexico

Mission Statement

Meet or Beat our Expectations!

School Characteristics:

Grade Levels: PreK–5

Locale: Town-remote

Total Students: 306

Male-Female Ratio: 48:52

Student-Teacher Ratio: 14.6:1

Free Lunch Eligible: 74.5%

Reduced-Price Lunch Eligible: 10.5%

Ethnicity	N	%
AmerInd/Alaskan	188	61.4
Asian	5	1.6
Black	0	0.0
Hispanic	103	33.7
White	10	3.3

General Information:

801 West Hill

Gallup, NM 87301

(505) 721-1051

http://lne.gmcs.k12.nm.us/

Parkside Elementary
Powell, Wyoming

Mission Statement

The Parkside Elementary Staff and parents will help each student acquire knowledge, skills, and attitudes to become:

Productive
Responsible
Inquisitive
Divergent
Evaluative

School Characteristics:

Grade Levels: K–5
Locale: Town-remote
Total Students: 236
Male-Female Ratio: 54:46
Student-Teacher Ratio: 13.9:1
Free Lunch Eligible: 31.4%
Reduced-Price Lunch Eligible: 15.7%

Ethnicity	N	%
AmerInd/Alaskan	0	0.0
Asian	1	0.4
Black	0	0.0
Hispanic	29	12.3
White	203	86.0
Two or more races	3	1.3

General Information:

160 North Evarts
Powell, WY 82435
(307) 754-5187
www.park1.net/Pages/Schools/Parkside.html

Providence Elementary School
Providence, Utah

Mission Statement

The mission of Providence Elementary School is to establish a cooperative school-wide community where children are eager to learn, are successful and happy; a school where children meet new challenges with confidence in their own self-worth and the worth of others.

School Characteristics:

Grade Levels: K–5
Locale: Suburb-small
Total Students: 692
Male-Female Ratio: 49:51
Student-Teacher Ratio: 33.0:1
Free Lunch Eligible: 11.3%
Reduced-Price Lunch Eligible: 12.0%

Ethnicity	N	%
AmerInd/Alaskan	0	0.0
Asian	11	1.9
Black	3	0.5
Hispanic	11	1.9
White	540	95.6

General Information:

91 East Center
Providence, UT 84332
(435) 752-6010
www.ccsdut.org/providence.cfm?subpage=24

Tombaugh Elementary School
Las Cruces, New Mexico

Mission Statement

As teachers at Tombaugh, we provide each student a differentiated education in a safe, encouraging environment that promotes self-discipline, motivation, and excellence in learning. We work with parents and community to support the students in developing skills to become successful adults.

School Characteristics:
Grade Levels: PreK–5
Locale: Suburb-midsize
Total Students: 672
Male-Female Ratio: 48:52
Student-Teacher Ratio: 16.3:1
Free Lunch Eligible: 58.5%
Reduced-Price Lunch Eligible: 6.3%

Ethnicity	N	%
AmerInd/Alaskan	1	0.1
Asian	5	0.7
Black	5	0.7
Hispanic	515	76.6
White	146	21.7

General Information:
226 Carver Road
Las Cruces, NM 88001
(505) 527-9575
http://tombaugh.lcps.k12.nm.us/
Schoolinfo.shtml

4

Public Middle Schools

The advent and increase of public middle schools in the United States represents one of the largest and most recent structural shifts in American education. In 1970, the US Department of Education reported just over 2,000 middle schools in the United States. Forty years later, more than 13,000 public middle schools are in operation across the country.

This large increase in American middle schools over the past four decades is a result of many elementary schools focusing exclusively on kindergarten through fifth grade, as well as an evolution of the junior high school. Whereas traditional junior high schools had previously served students in grades seven through nine, the middle school model typically serves grades six, seven, and eight, for children between the ages of eleven and thirteen. The philosophy of today's middle school has also evolved from previous junior high models to better serve the unique needs of students during adolescence.

As contrasted with the common elementary model of the self-contained classroom, students in most middle schools typically travel from class to class and multiple teachers are trained as specialists in a specific subject area. Unlike previous junior high school models, groups of teachers are organized by grade level so that "teams" or "clusters" of teachers often work collaboratively with a single cohort of students. As with elementary schools, the determination of which public middle school students attend is largely driven by geographic boundaries, and school funding is supported by local property taxes.

Source: US Department of Education, National Center for Education Statistics (2010).

Beresford Middle School
Beresford, South Dakota

Mission Statement

Dedicated to enhancing the learning process that starts now and lasts a lifetime.

School Characteristics:

Grade Levels: 6–8
Locale: Rural-remote
Total Students: 143
Male-Female Ratio: 52:48
Student-Teacher Ratio: 14.6:1
Free Lunch Eligible: 14.7%
Reduced-Price Lunch Eligible: 10.4%

Ethnicity	N	%
AmerInd/Alaskan	2	1.4
Asian	2	1.4
Black	0	0.0
Hispanic	2	1.4
White	137	95.8

General Information:

205 West Maple
Beresford, SD 57004
(605) 763-2139
http://beresford.schoolwires.net/Domain/9

Glen Crest Middle School
Glen Ellyn, Illinois

Mission Statement

Glen Crest Middle School is dedicated to creating an environment that prepares students to be responsible and respectful life-long learners, and empowers its students, staff, and parents to learn, work, and grow together in an ever-changing world.

School Characteristics:

Grade Levels: 6–8
Locale: Suburb-large
Total Students: 732
Male-Female Ratio: 49:51
Student-Teacher Ratio: 14.2:1
Free Lunch Eligible: 0%
Reduced-Price Lunch Eligible: 0%

Ethnicity	N	%
AmerInd/Alaskan	0	0.0
Asian	88	12.4
Black	75	10.6
Hispanic	60	8.5
White	487	68.6

General Information:

725 Sheehan Ave
Glen Ellyn, IL 60137
(630) 469-5220
www.ccsd89.org/index.php?option=com_content&task=blogcategory&id=28&Itemid=139

Henry J. McLaughlin Jr. Middle School
Manchester, New Hampshire

Mission Statement

McLaughlin Middle School is a school that understands the intellectual, physical, social, and emotional needs of pre and early adolescents, cares for them and prepares them for academic success. These future citizens are the life blood, hope and future of this city, the nation, and the world. We recognize that it is our responsibility to provide the future generations with an education that will meet their needs in a constantly changing world. We also affirm that the process of education is a partnership between students, education, parents, and the community and is based on mutual respect and cooperation. Education is the development of the whole person which includes intellectual, social, physical and emotional components. The school recognizes the individual abilities, differences, and interest of students and attempts to provide ways for them to understand themselves; to develop self-discipline, self-confidence, and a good self image; to develop their entire person to the epitome of their abilities, ever striving to achieve high standards and worthy goals.

School Characteristics:
Grade Levels: 6–8
Locale: City-midsize
Total Students: 783
Male-Female Ratio: 50:50
Student-Teacher Ratio: 13.1:1
Free Lunch Eligible: 39.6%
Reduced-Price Lunch Eligible: 6.0%

Ethnicity	N	%
AmerInd/Alaskan	0	0.0
Asian	28	3.6
Black	84	10.7
Hispanic	109	13.9
White	562	71.8

General Information:
290 South Mammoth Road
Manchester, NH 03109
(603) 628-6247
www.manchesternh.gov/website/Departments/PublicSchools/
Administration/Schools/Middle/McLaughlin/OurSchool/
MissionandVision/tabid/2020/Default.aspx

Kingsley Junior High School
Normal, Illinois

McLean County Unit 5 Schools Mission Statement

Unit 5 will educate each student to achieve personal excellence.

School Characteristics:

Grade Levels: 6–8
Locale: City-small
Total Students: 1,008
Male-Female Ratio: 49:51
Student-Teacher Ratio: 14.3:1
Free Lunch Eligible: 22.4%
Reduced-Price Lunch Eligible: 4.6%

Ethnicity	N	%
AmerInd/Alaskan	7	0.7
Asian	58	6.1
Black	138	14.6
Hispanic	51	5.4
White	692	73.2

General Information:

303 Kingsley
Normal, IL 61761
(309) 452-4461
www.unit5.org/kjhs/index.php

Dr. Martin Luther King, Jr. Middle School
Germantown, Maryland

Mission Statement

The mission of the Dr. Martin Luther King, Jr. Middle School community is a commitment to working together to eliminate the racial predictability of student achievement.

School Characteristics:

Grade Levels: 6–8
Locale: Suburb-large
Total Students: 577
Male-Female Ratio: 51:49
Student-Teacher Ratio: 14.1:1
Free Lunch Eligible: 27.9%
Reduced-Price Lunch Eligible: 11.1%

Ethnicity	N	%
AmerInd/Alaskan	4	0.7
Asian	74	12.8
Black	182	31.5
Hispanic	137	23.7
White	180	31.2

General Information:

13737 Wisteria Drive
Germantown, MD 20874
(301) 353-8080
www.montgomeryschoolsmd.org/schools/mlkms/aboutus/

Princeton Middle School
Princeton, West Virginia

Mission Statement

To offer all students: an education within a safe environment that will enhance and improve their academic and personal lives by incorporating 21st Century teaching skills.

School Characteristics:

Grade Levels: 6–8
Locale: Town-remote
Total Students: 616
Male-Female Ratio: 50:50
Student-Teacher Ratio: 13.4:1
Free Lunch Eligible: 43.3%
Reduced-Price Lunch Eligible: 8.0%

Ethnicity	N	%
AmerInd/Alaskan	0	0.0
Asian	9	1.5
Black	53	8.6
Hispanic	3	0.5
White	548	89.0
Two or more races	3	0.5

General Information:

300 North Johnston Street
Princeton, WV 24740
(304) 425-7517
http://pms.merc.k12.wv.us/

Sioux Valley Middle School
Volga, South Dakota

Mission Statement

Preparing individuals to succeed in an ever-changing global community.

School Characteristics:

Grade Levels: 6–8

Locale: Rural-remote

Total Students: 118

Male-Female Ratio: 47:53

Student-Teacher Ratio: 13.4:1

Free Lunch Eligible: 13.6%

Reduced-Price Lunch Eligible: 5.9%

Ethnicity	N	%
AmerInd/Alaskan	0	0.0
Asian	2	1.7
Black	0	0.0
Hispanic	0	0.0
White	116	98.3

General Information:

PO Box 278

Volga, SD 57071

(605) 627-5657

www.svs.k12.sd.us/

Timberlane Regional Middle School
Plaistow, New Hampshire

Mission Statement

The Timberlane Regional Middle School is committed to sustaining a collaborative learning environment so that our students may become successful, independent learners. It is our mission to:

- ◆ Provide a safe, respectful, and nurturing environment that encourages enthusiasm for learning.
- ◆ Foster responsible citizenship and provide opportunities for students to acquire and demonstrate leadership and service.
- ◆ Provide a challenging, integrated, standards-based curriculum.
- ◆ Meet the individual needs of students by identifying differences and using assessment to differentiate instruction and learning.

School Characteristics:
Grade Levels: 6–8
Locale: Suburb-large
Total Students: 1,077
Male-Female Ratio: 52:48
Student-Teacher Ratio: 11.6:1
Free Lunch Eligible: 8.8%
Reduced-Price Lunch Eligible: 5.8%

Ethnicity	N	%
AmerInd/Alaskan	1	0.1
Asian	6	0.6
Black	18	1.7
Hispanic	8	0.7
White	1,044	96.9

General Information:
44 Greenough Road
Plaistow, NH 03865
(603) 382-7131
www.timberlanems.com/

Tremont Middle School
Tremont, Illinois

Mission Statement

The mission of Tremont Middle School is to provide a positive environment incorporating meaningful and challenging activities designed to instill a desire for life long learning.

School Characteristics:

Grade Levels: 5–8

Locale: Rural-fringe

Total Students: 317

Male-Female Ratio: 54:46

Student-Teacher Ratio: 17.3:1

Free Lunch Eligible: 7.0%

Reduced-Price Lunch Eligible: 2.6%

Ethnicity	N	%
AmerInd/Alaskan	0	0
Asian	1	0.3
Black	2	0.7
Hispanic	5	1.6
White	296	97.4

General Information:

400 West Pearl

Tremont, IL 61568

(309) 925-3823

http://tremont.il.schoolwebpages.com/education/school/school.php?sectionid=4

Westwood Middle School
Morgantown, West Virginia

Mission Statement

The staff of Westwood Middle School will provide a safe, equitable learning environment that will strive for the success of all of our students. We believe that by creating and continuing this positive atmosphere, we will be promoting one's self worth and accomplishments while providing high expectations for all. This atmosphere will also enhance a positive attitude toward school and school-community involvement.

School Characteristics:

Grade Levels: 6–8
Locale: Rural-fringe
Total Students: 418
Male-Female Ratio: 51:49
Student-Teacher Ratio: 12.3:1
Free Lunch Eligible: 43.0%
Reduced-Price Lunch Eligible: 15.1%

Ethnicity	N	%
AmerInd/Alaskan	0	0.0
Asian	3	0.7
Black	29	6.9
Hispanic	2	0.5
White	384	91.9

General Information:

670 River Road
Morgantown, WV 26501
(304) 291-9300
http://boe.mono.k12.wv.us/westwood/

Windham Middle School
Windham, New Hampshire

Mission Statement

Windham Middle School is committed to providing a safe learning environment. Individuals are encouraged to be life long learners, respectful of themselves and others, and challenged to maximize their growth emotionally, socially, and intellectually.

School Characteristics:

Grade Levels: 6–8
Locale: Rural-fringe
Total Students: 613
Male-Female Ratio: 49:51
Student-Teacher Ratio: 13.6:1
Free Lunch Eligible: 3.4%
Reduced-Price Lunch Eligible: 2.3%

Ethnicity	N	%
AmerInd/Alaskan	1	0.2
Asian	18	2.9
Black	5	0.8
Hispanic	7	1.1
White	582	94.9

General Information:

112A Lowell Road
Windham, NH 03087
(603) 893-2636
www.windhamsd.org/wms/index.cfm

5

Public High Schools

Nearly 19,000 high schools with a twelfth-grade enrollment of at least fifteen students can be found in the United States. Currently, an estimated 16.4 million students are enrolled in US high schools. Individual states set the compulsory attendance age requirements for high school, typically between sixteen and eighteen years old.

Individual states and regions exhibit variations in the grade, student, and staff configurations of high schools across the country. Traditionally, most US high schools serve grades nine through twelve (children ages fourteen to eighteen). According to the US Department of Education, more than 16,000 public high schools serve at least grades ten, eleven, and twelve, in addition to 3,800 five-year or six-year public schools also serving grades seven and eight. In larger school systems, high schools are commonly further divided, with grades nine and ten separated from grades eleven and twelve, which is then known as senior high school.

Although there are state and regional differences, most US high schools include at least the following curricular foci for their students: English language arts, mathematics, science, social studies (which often includes US and world history, government, and economics), and physical education/health. As with the public elementary and middle schools, public high schools are funded by local property taxes, and residency typically determines which schools students attend.

The mission statements reproduced below represent those of a wide range of American high schools and illustrate variations in the scope and mission of our nation's diploma-granting institutions.

Sources: US Department of Education, National Center for Education Statistics (n.d.); US Department of Education, National Center for Education Statistics (2010); US News (2009).

Bentonville High School
Bentonville, Arkansas

Mission Statement

The mission of Bentonville High School is to provide our students with opportunities to obtain the skills needed to become productive, responsible citizens, capable of making positive contributions to a changing society.

School Characteristics:

Grade Levels: 9–12
Locale: City-small
Total Students: 3,333
Male-Female Ratio: 50:50
Student-Teacher Ratio: 16.4:1
Free Lunch Eligible: 16.9%
Reduced-Price Lunch Eligible: 6.5%

Ethnicity	N	%
AmerInd/Alaskan	54	1.6
Asian	94	2.8
Black	81	2.4
Hispanic	386	11.6
White	2,630	78.9
Two or more races	88	2.6

General Information:

1801 SE J Street
Bentonville, AR 72712
(479) 254-5100
http://bentonvillek12.org/bhs/about.asp

Bellows Free Academy
Fairfax, Vermont

Mission Statement

Committed to ensuring all students become informed, literate, critical thinkers who demonstrate responsible social and civic behaviors.

School Characteristics:

Grade Levels: 9–12
Locale: Rural-fringe
Total Students: 398
Male-Female Ratio: 52:48
Student-Teacher Ratio: 12.1:1
Free Lunch Eligible: 13.6%
Reduced-Price Lunch Eligible: 4.3%

Ethnicity	N	%
AmerInd/Alaskan	6	1.5
Asian	3	0.8
Black	3	0.8
Hispanic	5	1.3
White	371	93.2
Two or more races	10	2.5

General Information:

75 Hunt Street
Fairfax, VT 05454
(802) 849-6711
http://bfa.fwsu.schoolfusion.us/modules/cms/announce
.phtml?sessionid=65d3e721f4ee8aa821657936bf7cfda5&sessionid=
65d3e721f4ee8aa821657936bf7cfda5

Billings West High School
Billings, Montana

Mission Statement

Billings West High School commits to providing educational excellence by empowering students with the means for success and by challenging them to become productive citizens.

School Characteristics:

Grade Levels: 9–12
Locale: City-midsize
Total Students: 1,956
Male-Female Ratio: 50:50
Student-Teacher Ratio: 14.9:1
Free Lunch Eligible: 12.1%
Reduced-Price Lunch Eligible: 4.7%

Ethnicity	N	%
AmerInd/Alaskan	89	4.5
Asian	33	1.7
Black	25	1.3
Hispanic	68	3.5
White	1,741	89.0

General Information:

2201 St. John's Avenue
Billings, MT 59102
(406) 281-5600
http://billingswest.billings.k12.mt.us/

Bossier High School
Bossier City, Louisiana

Mission Statement

The Mission of Bossier High School, in partnership with parents and community, is to foster the development of an environment that will facilitate learning for all students, promote self-esteem and respect for others, and launch learners on a quest for high standards, all of which will lead them to be self-sufficient adults.

School Characteristics:

Grade Levels: 9–12
Locale: City-small
Total Students: 647
Male-Female Ratio: 48:52
Student-Teacher Ratio: 14.1:1
Free Lunch Eligible: 57.6%
Reduced-Price Lunch Eligible: 10.2%

Ethnicity	N	%
AmerInd/Alaskan	1	0.2
Asian	16	2.5
Black	389	60.1
Hispanic	73	11.3
White	168	26.0

General Information:

777 Bearkat Drive
Bossier City, LA 71111
(318) 549-6680
http://bossierh-bps-la.schoolloop.com/

Hellgate High School
Missoula, Montana

Mission Statement

Hellgate High School, in partnership with students, parents, and the community, will provide a rigorous education in a safe environment through which students can acquire knowledge, skills, and behaviors needed to fulfill their adult roles and responsibilities in the twenty-first century.

School Characteristics:

Grade Levels: 9–12
Locale: City-small
Total Students: 1,251
Male-Female Ratio: 50:50
Student-Teacher Ratio: 13.9:1
Free Lunch Eligible: 25.6%
Reduced-Price Lunch Eligible: 7.6%

Ethnicity	N	%
AmerInd/Alaskan	57	4.6
Asian	23	1.8
Black	5	0.4
Hispanic	21	1.7
White	1,145	91.5

General Information:

900 Higgins Avenue
Missoula, MT 59801
(406) 728-2402
www.mcps.k12.mt.us/portal/Default.aspx?alias=www.mcps.k12.mt.us/portal/hhs

Montpelier High School
Montpelier, Vermont

Mission Statement

Students will be capable, motivated contributors to their local, national, and world communities.

School Characteristics:

Grade Levels: 9–12
Locale: Town-remote
Total Students: 324
Male-Female Ratio: 49:51
Student-Teacher Ratio: 8.4:1
Free Lunch Eligible: 16.7%
Reduced-Price Lunch Eligible: 2.5%

Ethnicity	N	%
AmerInd/Alaskan	2	0.6
Asian	11	3.4
Black	4	1.2
Hispanic	9	2.8
White	291	89.8
Two or more races	7	2.2

General Information:

5 High School Drive
Montpelier, VT 05602
(802) 225-8000
www.mpsvt.org/mhs

Rutland Senior High School
Rutland, Vermont

Mission Statement

In partnership with students, parents and community, Rutland High School offers diverse learning opportunities and strives to meet the academic, social, physical and emotional needs of all its students. We provide a safe, orderly, healthy environment that is conducive to teaching and learning and a school climate that values mutual respect and dignity. Rutland High School graduates will possess the skills and knowledge necessary to be life-long learners and productive citizens.

School Characteristics:

Grade Levels: 9–12
Locale: Town-remote
Total Students: 1,038
Male-Female Ratio: 50:50
Student-Teacher Ratio: 10.5:1
Free Lunch Eligible: 26.8%
Reduced-Price Lunch Eligible: 5.1%

Ethnicity	N	%
AmerInd/Alaskan	0	0.0
Asian	6	0.6
Black	6	0.6
Hispanic	16	1.5
White	1,000	96.3
Two or more races	10	1.0

General Information:

22 Stratton Rd
Rutland, VT 05701
(802) 773-1955
http://rhs.rutlandcitypublicschools.org/about-2/

South High School
Fargo, North Dakota

Mission Statement

Students will be self-reliant people of sound character who have highly developed academic, communication and life skills to succeed in their own lives while contributing to the well-being of their communities.

School Characteristics:

Grade Levels: 9–12
Locale: City-small
Total Students: 2,113
Male-Female Ratio: 50:50
Student-Teacher Ratio: 14.9:1
Free Lunch Eligible: 15.0%
Reduced-Price Lunch Eligible: 4.6%

Ethnicity	N	%
AmerInd/Alaskan	42	2.0
Asian	52	2.5
Black	127	6.0
Hispanic	47	2.2
White	1,845	87.3

General Information:

1840 15th Ave South
Fargo, ND 58103
(701) 446-2000
www.fargo.k12.nd.us/education/school/school.php?sectionid=154

Winooski High School
Winooski, Vermont

Mission Statement

To continually challenge our students to develop as responsible citizens.

School Characteristics:

Grade Levels: 9–12
Locale: Suburb-midsize
Total Students: 267
Male-Female Ratio: 58:42
Student-Teacher Ratio: 10.7:1
Free Lunch Eligible: 61.4%
Reduced-Price Lunch Eligible: 10.1%

Ethnicity	N	%
AmerInd/Alaskan	1	0.4
Asian	23	8.6
Black	73	27.3
Hispanic	2	0.7
White	164	61.4
Two or more races	4	1.5

General Information:

60 Normand St.
Winooski, VT 05404
(802) 655-3530
www.winooski.k12.vt.us/2076101020115450417/blank/browse.asp?a=383&
BMDRN=2000&BCOB=0&c=56145&2076101020115450417Nav=|&NodeID=
237

Wynne High School
Wynne, Arkansas

Mission Statement

The staff of Wynne High School believes that all students have potential, and we strive to challenge all students to maximize their educational abilities.

School Characteristics:

Grade Levels: 9–12
Locale: Town-remote
Total Students: 895
Male-Female Ratio: 50:50
Student-Teacher Ratio: 13.4:1
Free Lunch Eligible: 39.2%
Reduced-Price Lunch Eligible: 10.5%

Ethnicity	N	%
AmerInd/Alaskan	2	0.2
Asian	17	1.9
Black	290	32.4
Hispanic	11	1.2
White	575	64.2

General Information:

800 East Jackson Street
Wynne, AR 72396
(870) 238-5000
http://wynne.k12.ar.us/hs/

6

Vocational/Career/Technical Education Schools

According to the US Department of Education, approximately 900 full-time vocational (also known as career/technical education) public high schools serve US students. Thus, about 5 percent of public high schools are devoted exclusively to vocational/CT education. However, vocational/CT education is also frequently embedded into traditional public high schools, where approximately 88 percent offer some form of vocational program on- or off-site. Indeed, more than 90 percent of public high school students currently complete at least some credits in occupational course work through their own school (typically in technology or business). However, this chapter focuses exclusively on the mission statements of the full-time US vocational high schools.

Vocational and CT education schools offer a wide range of training that reflects the transformations of the American economy and workforce over the last generation. At many vocational high schools, students participate in a course of study that includes traditional core academic courses (ELA, math, social studies, science). In addition, students participate in courses designed to strengthen their general labor market skills and provide introductory computer skills in addition to a student's specific trade or occupational specialization.

Among the most common career and technical education specializations offered by vocational high schools are agriculture; business management and service; marketing technology and communication; construction; mechanics, repair, and automotive; transportation; materials production; print production; health care; child care and education; food service and hospitality; personal and health care.

In addition, some schools offer students life enrichment programs targeting family and consumer life skills for those students not pursuing postsecondary education or the paid labor market. The mission statements reproduced below illustrate a variety of vocational high schools in America in the early 21st century.

Sources: Association for Career and Technical Education (2011); Levesque, Laird, Hensley, Choy, Cataldi, & Hudson (2008); RWM.org: Vocational Schools Database (2011); US Department of Education, National Center for Education Statistics (2008); US Department of Education (2011b).

Mercy Vocational High School
Philadelphia, Pennsylvania

Mission Statement

Mercy Vocational High School is a private, urban vocational high school sponsored by the Sisters of Mercy. The school's mission is to provide a Catholic education to those students whose educational and career goals are best served by a quality, comprehensive academic/vocational secondary school program. Students acquire marketable skills to enter immediately into their career vocation or to pursue post-secondary education. As a school Community we seek to live the Gospel in word and action. We place the highest priority on the spiritual and moral development of our students and their service to others.

School Characteristics:

Grade Levels: 9–12
Locale: City-large
Total Students: 373
Male-Female Ratio: N/A
Student-Teacher Ratio: 10.4:1
Free Lunch Eligible: N/A
Reduced-Price Lunch Eligible: N/A

Ethnicity	N	%
AmerInd/Alaskan	1	0.3
Asian	4	1.1
Black	149	39.9
Hispanic	43	11.5
White	176	47.2

General Information:

2900 West Hunting Park Avenue
Philadelphia, PA 19129
(215) 226-1225
www.mercyvocational.org/

Nature Coast Technical High School
Brooksville, Florida

Mission Statement

Nature Coast Technical High School's mission is to equip students with skills in technology, problem solving, critical thinking and social interactions by developing an atmosphere of trust, high expectations and consistent support. Our success will be measured through student achievement of maximum potential; parental, community, and employer satisfaction with our students; and improvement on standardized tests such as the FCAT, ACT and SAT.

School Characteristics:

Grade Levels: 9–12
Locale: Suburb-midsize
Total Students: 1,497
Male-Female Ratio: 49:51
Student-Teacher Ratio: 15.7:1
Free Lunch Eligible: 24.2%
Reduced-Price Lunch Eligible: 11.8%

Ethnicity	N	%
AmerInd/Alaskan	3	0.2
Asian	14	1.0
Black	96	6.6
Hispanic	196	13.6
White	1,135	78.6

General Information:

4057 California Street
Brooksville, FL 34604
(352) 797-7088
www.edline.net/pages/HCSB_NCTHS

North County Trade Tech School
Vista, California

Mission Statement

To graduate students with a strong blend of academic and workforce competencies necessary for future success in post-secondary education and in the building and construction industry.

School Characteristics:

Grade Levels: 9–12
Locale: Rural-fringe
Total Students: 41
Male-Female Ratio: 97:3
Student-Teacher Ratio: 8.2:1
Free Lunch Eligible: 51.2%
Reduced-Price Lunch Eligible: 0%

Ethnicity	N	%
AmerInd/Alaskan	0	0.0
Asian	2	4.9
Black	1	2.4
Hispanic	16	39.0
White	16	39.0
Two or more races	6	14.6

General Information:

1126 North Melrose Drive
Vista, CA 92083
(760) 598-0782
www.tradetechhigh.org/

Oakland Technical High School
Oakland, California

Mission Statement

All members of the Tech community will work cooperatively and communicate respectfully in a peaceful, safe and clean environment. All Tech students will strive to achieve high expectations, meet solid academic standards, and have equal access to an enriching curriculum that will enable them to reach their highest potential. All Tech students will graduate with strong academic, vocational, and social skills, prepared to enter college, quality jobs and career training.

School Characteristics:

Grade Levels: 9–12
Locale: City-large
Total Students: 1,741
Male-Female Ratio: 52:48
Student-Teacher Ratio: 20.2:1
Free Lunch Eligible: 47.3%
Reduced-Price Lunch Eligible: 9.1%

Ethnicity	N	%
AmerInd/Alaskan	4	0.2
Asian	330	19.3
Black	898	52.4
Hispanic	253	14.8
White	167	9.7
Two or more races	62	3.6

General Information:

4351 Broadway
Oakland, CA 94611
(510) 879-3050
http://oaklandtech.com/

Paul M. Hodgson Vocational Technical High School
Newark, Delaware

Mission Statement

Our mission is to prepare students vocationally and academically to be productive, employable citizens of society by integrating high quality instruction and technology in a safe, caring, and cooperative school environment.

School Characteristics:

Grade Levels: 8–12
Locale: Suburb-large
Total Students: 1,230
Male-Female Ratio: 56:44
Student-Teacher Ratio: 16.4:1
Free Lunch Eligible: 12.2%
Reduced-Price Lunch Eligible: 5.1%

Ethnicity	N	%
AmerInd/Alaskan	1	0.1
Asian	12	1.0
Black	377	30.7
Hispanic	78	6.3
White	762	62.0

General Information:

2575 Glasgow Avenue
Newark, DE 19702
(302) 834-0990
www.nccvthighschools.com/HODGSON/index.php

Pierson Vocational High School
Nogales, Arizona

Mission Statement

Pierson Vocational High School's Philosophy is to Inspire all Students to Develop Marketable 21st Century Skills. These Skills Include Reading, Writing, Mathematics, Computer Knowledge, Collaboration and the Integrity of Being a Responsible and Productive Citizen.

School Characteristics:

Grade Levels: 9–12
Locale: Town-remote
Total Students: 134
Male-Female Ratio: 60:40
Student-Teacher Ratio: 13.4:1
Free Lunch Eligible: 82.8%
Reduced-Price Lunch Eligible: 8.2%

Ethnicity	N	%
AmerInd/Alaskan	0	0.0
Asian	0	0.0
Black	0	0.0
Hispanic	133	99.25
White	1	0.75

General Information:

310 W. Plum St.
Nogales, AZ 85621
(520) 287-0800
http://pvhsprincipal.jimdo.com/

Queens Vocational and Technical High School
Queens, New York

Mission Statement

Queens Vocational & Technical High School is committed to preparing our students with the critical thinking, problem solving and team building skills necessary to meet the demands of a highly technical and ever expanding global economy. Our dual mission is to graduate students who are not only ready for post-secondary education, but who can also readily integrate into our work force as skilled, productive, contributing citizens. Our students are prepared to succeed.

School Characteristics:

Grade Levels: 9–12
Locale: City-large
Total Students: 1,218
Male-Female Ratio: 61:39
Student-Teacher Ratio: 17.6:1
Free Lunch Eligible: 59.9%
Reduced-Price Lunch Eligible: 13.3%

Ethnicity	N	%
AmerInd/Alaskan	1	0.1
Asian	111	9.1
Black	124	10.2
Hispanic	852	70.0
White	130	10.7

General Information:

37-02 47 Avenue
Queens, NY 11101
(718) 937-3010
http://schools.nyc.gov/SchoolPortals/24/Q600/default.htm

Region 10 Vocational High School
Brunswick, Maine

Mission Statement

We teach technical skills, and work to enhance positive attitudes needed by students entering the competitive job market or post-secondary education. As always, enrollment at Region Ten is voluntary.

School Characteristics:

Grade Levels: 11–12
Locale: Rural-fringe
Total Students: N/A
Male-Female Ratio: N/A
Student-Teacher Ratio: N/A
Free Lunch Eligible: N/A
Reduced-Price Lunch Eligible: N/A

General Information:

68 Church Road
Brunswick, ME 04011
(207) 729-6622
http://region10.mainecte.org

Student population data not available from the CCD or Greatschools.net.

Smith Vocational and Agricultural High School
Northampton, Massachusetts

Mission Statement

Based on our proud heritage of both experimental and practical education, as established in 1844 by the Vision and Will of Oliver Smith, the mission of Smith Vocational and Agricultural High School is to educate students in an integrated program in the art and science of agriculture and other technical careers, and to provide experiential learning opportunities that will enable students to function proficiently within the parameters of the workplace and post-secondary education.

School Characteristics:

Grade Levels: 9–12
Locale: Suburb-large
Total Students: 460
Male-Female Ratio: 65:35
Student-Teacher Ratio: 8.6:1
Free Lunch Eligible: 23.7%
Reduced-Price Lunch Eligible: 9.3%

Ethnicity	N	%
AmerInd/Alaskan	2	0.4
Asian	5	1.1
Black	4	0.9
Hispanic	42	9.1
White	406	88.3
Two or more races	1	0.2

General Information:

80 Locust Street
Northampton, MA 01060
(413) 587-1414
http://smith.tec.ma.us/

7

Magnet Schools

Magnet schools are public schools whose aim is to draw in students based on the students' interests. Each magnet school has a specialized curricular focus or course offering that diverges in some way from those offered at traditional public schools. For example, some magnet schools focus on business topics (e.g., finance, leadership), whereas others focus intensively on technology or foreign languages.

Magnet schools exist at every level—elementary, middle, and high school—and are most often able to draw students from beyond the conventional district borders. In some cases, magnet schools are established as specialty programs within a larger school (e.g., a large high school may have a magnet school component that focuses on agriculture).

Some magnet schools require competitive admissions testing for students to enroll, whereas others select students based upon a lottery pick of students who have indicated their interest in attending the school.

The history of magnet schools dates back to the 1960s and is linked to the school desegregation movement. The goal was to create public schools that were so attractive (e.g., "magnetic") to students that parents of all ethnicities would voluntarily send their children to the schools because of the outstanding and unique programming. Thus, the intention was to foster desegregation via parental choice rather than forced desegregation (e.g., busing). Magnet schools have often been heralded as a model for achieving racial integration and high academic achievement.

Magnet schools are often confused with charter schools; however, magnet schools are distinctive since they typically operate within the public school bureaucracy (i.e., they are not independent). School districts fund magnet schools in the same way they fund other public schools. There are approximately 4,000 magnet and theme-based schools across the United States, and they are most frequently located in large cities.

Sources: Chen (2007); Magnet Schools of America (2007).

A. B. Combs Elementary Leadership Magnet School
Raleigh, North Carolina

Mission Statement

To develop global leaders one child at a time.

School Characteristics:

Grade Levels: K–5

Locale: City-large

Total Students: 820

Male-Female Ratio: 52:48

Student-Teacher Ratio: 13.6:1

Free Lunch Eligible: N/A

Reduced-Price Lunch Eligible: N/A

Ethnicity	N	%
AmerInd/Alaskan	1	0.1
Asian	62	7.6
Black	252	30.7
Hispanic	112	13.7
White	393	47.9

General Information:

2001 Lorimer Road

Raleigh, NC 27606

(919) 233-4300

http://combses.wcpss.net/node/19

Academic Magnet High School
North Charleston, South Carolina

Mission Statement

The mission of the Academic Magnet High School is to challenge each student, teacher and parent with the high expectations of a rigorous curriculum. We provide a learning environment that thoroughly prepares students for college and develops their self-esteem. Our students are encouraged to be citizens of the world, to acquire a sense of global responsibility, and to cultivate a respect for cultural diversity.

School Characteristics:

Grade Levels: 9–12
Locale: City-small
Total Students: 592
Male-Female Ratio: 48:52
Student-Teacher Ratio: 14.7:1
Free Lunch Eligible: 3.8%
Reduced-Price Lunch Eligible: 2.7%

Ethnicity	N	%
AmerInd/Alaskan	4	0.7
Asian	72	12.3
Black	58	9.9
Hispanic	19	3.3
White	430	73.8

General Information:

5109-A West Enterprise Street
North Charleston, SC 29405
(843) 746-1300
http://amhs.ccsdschools.com

Advanced Technologies Academy
Las Vegas, Nevada

Mission Statement

The mission of Advanced Technologies Academy is to empower a diverse student body to succeed in a competitive world by promoting academic concepts, technological skills, and ethical behavior.

School Characteristics:

Grade Levels: 9–12
Locale: City-large
Total Students: 995
Male-Female Ratio: 59:41
Student-Teacher Ratio: 17.2:1
Free Lunch Eligible: 13.5%
Reduced-Price Lunch Eligible: 5.6%

Ethnicity	N	%
AmerInd/Alaskan	5	0.5
Asian	236	23.7
Black	86	8.6
Hispanic	221	22.2
White	447	44.9

General Information:

2501 Vegas Drive
Las Vegas, NV 89106
(702) 799-7870
www.atech.org/general-information/mascot-motto-mission-beliefs/

Carter Academy
Houston, Texas

Mission Statement

We will collaborate as a school community to provide the best instruction for every student in order to meet and exceed grade level expectations regardless of previous academic performance. It is our purpose and responsibility to educate all students to high levels of academic, social, and creative performance while fostering positive growth in social behaviors and attitudes.

School Characteristics:

Grade Levels: K–4
Locale: Suburb-large
Total Students: 790
Male-Female Ratio: 50:50
Student-Teacher Ratio: 11.9:1
Free Lunch Eligible: 72.8%
Reduced-Price Lunch Eligible: 13.4%

Ethnicity	N	%
AmerInd/Alaskan	0	0.0
Asian	10	1.3
Black	212	26.8
Hispanic	552	69.9
White	16	2.0

General Information:

3111 Fallbrook
Houston, TX 77038
(281) 878-7760
http://schools.aldine.k12.tx.us/webs/107/home.htm

Forest Lake Elementary School
Columbia, South Carolina

Mission Statement

Our School, in partnership with families and the community, provides a safe, nurturing environment for the growth and development of young children. We accomplish this through a technology infused integrated curriculum that demands academic excellence, encourages positive self-esteem, and promotes responsible citizenship and respect for others.

School Characteristics:

Grade Levels: K–5
Locale: Suburb-large
Total Students: 577
Male-Female Ratio: 50:50
Student-Teacher Ratio: 12.0:1
Free Lunch Eligible: 43.7%
Reduced-Price Lunch Eligible: 9.0%

Ethnicity	N	%
AmerInd/Alaskan	1	0.2
Asian	15	2.6
Black	362	63.5
Hispanic	37	6.5
White	155	27.2

General Information:

6801 Brookfield Road
Columbia, SC 29206
(803) 782-0470
www.richland2.org/schools/fle/

McFatter Technical High School
Davie, Florida

Mission Statement

William T. McFatter Technical High School is committed to providing an education for ALL students that allows them the opportunity to achieve three primary goals.

1. Acceptance to a four-year university
2. Possible articulation into a Community College
3. Certification in a high wage, high demand Technical Area.

In order to achieve these goals every student is required to take a college preparatory curriculum of 24 credits predetermined by the school and an 8 credit course of study in a technical field selected by the student. We require the same 24 credits for all students. The 8 technical credits are studied in the junior and senior years.

School Characteristics:
Grade Levels: 9–12
Locale: Suburban-large
Total Students: 557
Male-Female Ratio: 52:48
Student-Teacher Ratio: 2.5:1
Free Lunch Eligible: 15.2%
Reduced-Price Lunch Eligible: 9.8%

Ethnicity	N	%
AmerInd/Alaskan	0	0.0
Asian	20	3.7
Black	90	16.6
Hispanic	202	37.3
White	229	42.3

General Information:
6500 Nova Drive
Davie, FL 33317
(754) 321-5700
http://mcfattertech-hs.com/index.html

Normal Park Museum Magnet
Chattanooga, Tennessee

Mission Statement

To instill lifelong intellectual curiosity, sound judgment and deep under-standing by building a solid educational foundation based on meaningful exploration and discovery. We shall accomplish this through collaborative partnerships with parents, museums, and the community in a unique, cre-ative and dynamic environment.

School Characteristics:

Grade Levels: PreK–8
Locale: City-midsize
Total Students: 523
Male-Female Ratio: 50:50
Student-Teacher Ratio: 10.9:1
Free Lunch Eligible: 19.3%
Reduced-Price Lunch Eligible: 1.7%

Ethnicity	N	%
AmerInd/Alaskan	4	0.8
Asian	8	1.5
Black	114	21.8
Hispanic	20	3.8
White	377	72.1

General Information:

1009 Mississippi Ave.
Chattanooga, TN 37405
(423) 209-5900
www.normalparkmuseummagnet.com/about-us/mission-core-values.aspx

Richard J. Kinsella Magnet School of Performing Arts
Hartford, Connecticut

Mission Statement

At the Richard J. Kinsella Magnet School of Performing Arts, we view each child as a competent and resourceful problem solver. Our mission is to provide each child with an enriched educational environment, which fosters artistic, independent and critical thinking through Arts integrated instruction. We are committed to celebrating student, staff, and community diversity while promoting life long learning, love of the Arts and developing persons of commendable moral character.

School Characteristics:

Grade Levels: PreK–8
Locale: City-midsize
Total Students: 569
Male-Female Ratio: 47:53
Student-Teacher Ratio: 10.5:1
Free Lunch Eligible: 99.5%
Reduced-Price Lunch Eligible: 0%

Ethnicity	N	%
AmerInd/Alaskan	2	0.4
Asian	5	0.9
Black	171	30.1
Hispanic	329	57.8
White	62	10.9

General Information:

65 Van Block Avenue
Hartford, CT 06106
(860) 695-4140
www.kmspa.org/about.shtml

Waterbury Arts Magnet School
Waterbury, Connecticut

Mission Statement

The Mission of the Waterbury Arts Magnet School is a safe learning environment with a strong academic curriculum partnered with a comprehensive arts curriculum. Through interaction with faculty, staff, peers, parents, and the community, a student's innate creativity and talents are nurtured in a secure educational setting. The Waterbury Arts Magnet School fosters respect for self and community as students are encouraged to fulfill their unique potentials. Students are prepared to pursue post-secondary studies or to join the workforce as civic-minded young adults.

> Academics and Arts
> Respect and Responsibility
> + Talent and Tolerance
> _____
> Skills for lifelong learning

School Characteristics:

Grade Levels: 6–12
Locale: Suburban-midsize
Total Students: 801
Male-Female Ratio: 41:59
Student-Teacher Ratio: 13.0:1
Free Lunch Eligible: 36.7%
Reduced-Price Lunch Eligible: 13.7%

Ethnicity	N	%
AmerInd/Alaskan	3	0.4
Asian	9	1.1
Black	217	27.1
Hispanic	164	20.5
White	408	50.9

General Information:

16 South Elm Street
Waterbury, CT 06706
(203) 573-6300
www.waterbury.k12.ct.us/wam/index.php

8

Charter Schools

Charter schools are a type of public school but are overseen by their own independent boards. In exchange for increased accountability, the schools are typically freed from many of the regulatory restrictions found in traditional public schools. "The 'charter' establishing each school is a performance contract detailing the schools' mission, goals, program, students served, methods of assessment, and ways to measure success" (National Charter School Resource Center, n.d.). Most charters are granted for a three- to five-year period and must be renewed at the end of each contract period. The charters are granted to the school by a sponsor—usually a state or local school board. Charter school leaders are ultimately accountable for the academic results and financial management of the school.

Charter schools are publicly funded by local, state, and federal tax dollars; however, many of these schools also raise money from private donors and federal and private grants. One of their defining features is that they are open to any parent who wishes to send their children there. Thus, charter schools have also become synonymous with school choice. Within the traditional public school system, a student attends the local area school; the determination about which school the child attends is based on the geographic location of the child's home. Charter schools offer an alternative public option that is not necessarily linked to any geographic restrictions. Charter schools are not allowed to charge tuition, and when more students are interested in attending a school than that school has slots available, the students are typically chosen using a random lottery process.

The second defining characteristic of charter schools is that most are designed to provide specialized curricular offerings that would not normally be found within the context of a traditional public school. For example, some charter schools focus on art and architecture; others focus on languages or technology.

The first charter school was opened in Minnesota in 1992; however, the concept of charter schools dates back to the 1960s. Today, more than one million students are enrolled in more than 5,700 charter schools across forty states and the District of Columbia (Center for Education Reform, 2011). To date, research on the effects of charter schools on student achievement has yielded mixed results (Center for Research on Educational Outcomes, 2009).

Sources: Center for Education Reform (2011); Center for Research on Educational Outcomes (2009); National Charter School Resource Center (n.d.).

Academy for Business and Leadership Education
St. Augustine, Florida

Mission Statement

ABLE will strive to inspire and cultivate the innate leadership and creative impulses within all children, developing educated, caring and responsible world citizens. This vision will be pursued at multiple learning sites to provide small, flexible learning communities in safe, challenging and caring educational environments. Innovative teaching strategies will emphasize enjoyable and relevant educational experiences in which the fundamentals of entrepreneurship and leadership will be integrated into all levels and subject areas. Students will master basic skills at a high level of competence while acquiring knowledge and skills in problem solving and decision-making. Our programs will be characterized by the cooperative presence and unified support of families, businesses, and educational and civic groups with whom our students will interact. Emphasis on self-sufficiency, civic responsibility and a passion for lifelong learning will develop responsible leaders for the 21st Century.

School Characteristics:

Grade Levels: 5–8
Locale: Suburb-small
Total Students: 125
Male-Female Ratio: 58:42
Student-Teacher Ratio: 17.9:1
Free Lunch Eligible: 0%
Reduced-Price Lunch Eligible: 0%

Ethnicity	N	%
AmerInd/Alaskan	0	0.0
Asian	1	0.8
Black	4	3.2
Hispanic	6	4.8
White	113	91.1

General Information:

7 Williams Street
St. Augustine, FL 32084
(904) 826-1606
http://ableschool.org/

Community Roots Charter School
Brooklyn, New York

Mission Statement

Community Roots Charter School is a rigorous K-5 learning community where learning is embedded in meaningful real world context, where children are deliberately taught to see the connections between school and the world. Community Roots students will meet or exceed the New York State standards and be prepared to excel in the 21st century by being taught to be independent thinkers and to work productively within a diverse group of learners. At Community Roots students learn to combine curiosity with appropriate application, which leads to deep understanding and the confidence to take on challenges to become who they want to be.

School Characteristics:

Grade Levels: K–4
Locale: City-large
Total Students: 202
Male-Female Ratio: 51:49
Student-Teacher Ratio: 9.6:1
Free Lunch Eligible: 26.7%
Reduced-Price Lunch Eligible: 8.4%

Ethnicity	N	%
AmerInd/Alaskan	3	1.7
Asian	1	0.6
Black	89	51.7
Hispanic	16	9.3
White	63	36.6

General Information:

51 Saint Edwards Street, Third Floor
Brooklyn, NY 11205
(718) 858-1629
www.communityroots.org/

Compass Charter School
Meridian, Idaho

Mission Statement

The Compass Public Charter School's mission is to prepare each child with a personal compass that will guide them in life's directions. We do so by developing students who are competent, confident, productive and responsible young adults who possess the habits, skills and attitudes to succeed in life and be offered the invitation of a post-secondary education and satisfying employment.

School Characteristics:

Grade Levels: K–11
Locale: Suburb-large
Total Students: 420
Male-Female Ratio: 53:47
Student-Teacher Ratio: 20.5:1
Free Lunch Eligible: 16.4%
Reduced-Price Lunch Eligible: 10.9%

Ethnicity	N	%
AmerInd/Alaskan	2	0.5
Asian	12	2.9
Black	5	1.2
Hispanic	11	2.6
White	390	92.9

General Information:

2511 West Cherry Lane
Meridian, ID 83642
(208) 855-2802
www.compasscharter.org/

Harding Fine Arts Academy
Oklahoma City, Oklahoma

Mission Statement

The mission of Harding Fine Arts Academy is to provide an arts enriched learning environment merging creative and academic content to enhance student achievement and to encourage arts related careers and lifelong arts appreciation.

School Characteristics:

Grade Levels: 9–12
Locale: City-large
Total Students: 208
Male-Female Ratio: 38:62
Student-Teacher Ratio: 13.8:1
Free Lunch Eligible: 47.0%
Reduced-Price Lunch Eligible: 9.4%

Ethnicity	N	%
AmerInd/Alaskan	12	5.8
Asian	10	4.8
Black	38	18.3
Hispanic	29	13.9
White	119	57.2

General Information:

3333 North Shartel
Oklahoma City, OK 73118
(405) 702-4322
http://hardingfinearts.org/

Jumoke Academy Charter Schools
Hartford, Connecticut

Mission Statement

The mission of Jumoke Academy Charter School is to prepare children to successfully compete in the global marketplace despite the social and economic challenges they may presently face. The academy is dedicated to rigorous academic and social standards achieved by holding high expectations for all students during challenging instruction.

The concept of "Jumoke" is central to the academy's mission to provide a safe and nurturing environment for its children while providing high quality instruction. Students in PreK–8th grade will be offered a developmentally appropriate curriculum and an enriched program of extended day activities which addresses the unique talents and background of each child in the areas of science, mathematics, language arts, technology, physical education, music and art enrichment.

School Characteristics:

Grade Levels: PreK–8
Locale: City-midsize
Total Students: 412
Male-Female Ratio: 45:55
Student-Teacher Ratio: 14.9:1
Free Lunch Eligible: 36.9%
Reduced-Price Lunch Eligible: 11.7%

Ethnicity	N	%
AmerInd/Alaskan	0	0.0
Asian	1	0.2
Black	398	96.6
Hispanic	13	3.2
White	0	0.0

General Information:

250 Blue Hills Avenue
Hartford, CT 06106
(860) 525-7758
http://jumokeacademy.org/

KIPP Academy of Opportunity
Los Angeles, California

Mission Statement

KAO's mission is to ensure that students develop the academic skills, character, and intellectual habits necessary to succeed in competitive high schools, colleges, and the world beyond. Our six guiding principles are: respect, hard work, results, constant learning, determination, and teamwork.

School Characteristics:

Grade Levels: 5–8
Locale: City-large
Total Students: 340
Male-Female Ratio: 51:49
Student-Teacher Ratio: 22.4:1
Free Lunch Eligible: 61.8%
Reduced-Price Lunch Eligible: 23.8%

Ethnicity	N	%
AmerInd/Alaskan	0	0.0
Asian	0	0.0
Black	299	87.9
Hispanic	41	12.1
White	0	0.0

General Information:

7019 South Van Ness Avenue
Los Angeles, CA 90047
(323) 778-0162
www.kippla.org/kao/

KIPP Sunshine Peak Academy
Denver, Colorado

Mission Statement

KSPA's goals for future college success focus on three components: academic skills, intellectual habits, and character traits. Students in each grade focus on one character trait per year to help them develop into successful adult citizens.

School Characteristics:

Grade Levels: 5–8

Locale: City-large

Total Students: 360

Male-Female Ratio: 46:54

Student-Teacher Ratio: 14.1:1

Free Lunch Eligible: 81.1%

Reduced-Price Lunch Eligible: 12.2%

Ethnicity	N	%
AmerInd/Alaskan	2	0.6
Asian	4	1.1
Black	7	1.9
Hispanic	341	94.7
White	6	1.7

General Information:

375 South Tejon Street

Denver, CO 80223

(303) 623-5772

www.kippcolorado.org/school/kipp-sunshine-peak-academy

Rilke Schule German School of Arts & Sciences
Anchorage, Alaska

Mission Statement

Rilke Schule German School of Arts & Sciences is a K through 8 public charter school that provides an outstanding education focused on high academic achievement by engaging each child through an enriched immersion language curriculum taught primarily in German.

School Characteristics:

Grade Levels: K–8
Locale: City-large
Total Students: 214
Male-Female Ratio: 52:48
Student-Teacher Ratio: 21.4:1
Free Lunch Eligible: 0%
Reduced-Price Lunch Eligible: 0%

General Information:

2511 Sentry Drive, Suite 100
Anchorage, AK 99507
(907) 742-7455
www.rilkeschule.org/

Ethnicity	N	%
AmerInd/Alaskan	2	0.9
Asian	6	2.8
Black	2	0.9
Hispanic	7	3.3
White	178	83.2
Two or more races	19	8.9

9

Native American/ Tribal Schools

Before the arrival of colonial settlers, an informal yet seemingly effective educational system served the inhabitants of North America for millennia. Since settlers arrived, the history of Native American and tribal schools in the US and Canada provides a chilling example of how education and schooling has been purposefully employed by state and federal policy makers as a powerful tool of cultural assimilation. For US policy makers, the purpose of the Native American schools was clear.

Beginning in the 19th century, policy makers at the Bureau of Indian Affairs promoted Indian boarding schools for "Americanizing" Native American student populations. Students at the schools were forbidden to wear traditional clothing, speak traditional languages, and engage in their cultural heritage. The curriculum included indoctrination of Christianity; European-American values; reading, writing, and speaking English; and job skills better suited to urban environments than traditional rural economies. In 1973, about 60,000 American Indian children attended Indian boarding schools. By 2007, this number had dropped to 9,500.

Today, most Native American children attend non-boarding school on more than 550 federally recognized reservations or in traditional public schools across the country. In the past forty years, both society and government policy have better recognized the unique heritage and cultural value and status of Native Americans. With federal assimilation programs officially abandoned, Native American and tribal schools have sought to reintegrate traditional Native American values and curricula. There remain formidable challenges defining the goals and purposes for the next generation of native students in this country. Currently, 36 percent of Native American students drop out after tenth grade, more than double the rate of students of European descent. Examples of mission statements in this chapter highlight school efforts to balance various forms of Native American values and traditions with the modern emphases of academic development.

Sources: Colmant (2000); Hammerschlag, Alderfer, & Berg (1973); TribalBiz.com (n.d.); Wikipedia Foundation (2007); Yeboah (2005).

Chief Leschi Schools
Puyallup, Washington

Mission Statement

Chief Leschi Schools' mission in cooperation with the Puyallup Tribe, the Native American community and the community as a greater whole is to create challenging opportunities to educate students in an atmosphere of mutual trust and respect. It is our common mission to inspire each student to achieve personal growth and cultural pride, to value life long learning, and to become a responsible contributing citizen of their community, the Puyallup Nation, Washington State, and the United States of America in a complex and ever changing world.

School Characteristics:

Grade Levels: K–12
Locale: N/A
Total Students: 770
Male-Female Ratio: 50:50
Student-Teacher Ratio: 12.2:1
Free Lunch Eligible: N/A
Reduced-Price Lunch Eligible: N/A

Ethnicity	N	%
AmerInd/Alaskan	770	100.0
Asian	0	0.0
Black	0	0.0
Hispanic	0	0.0
White	0	0.0

General Information:

5625 52nd Street East
Puyallup, WA 98371
(253) 445-6003
www.leschischools.org/

Gila Crossing Community School
Laveen, Arizona

Mission Statement

Work together to promote academic excellence. Honor the teachings of our elders, culture, and environment. Promote safe and healthy learning environment.

School Characteristics:

Grade Levels: PreK–8
Locale: Rural[1]
Total Students: 492
Male-Female Ratio: 50:50
Student-Teacher Ratio: 14.5:1
Free Lunch Eligible: N/A
Reduced-Price Lunch Eligible: N/A

Ethnicity	N	%
AmerInd/Alaskan	492	100.0
Asian	0	0.0
Black	0	0.0
Hispanic	0	0.0
White	0	0.0

General Information:

4665 West Pecos Road
Laveen, AZ 85339
(520) 550-4834
www.gccseagles.org/

[1]Locale not classified by CCD.

Kayenta Middle School
Kayenta, Arizona

Mission Statement

It is the individual's responsibility to attain a successful life. Thinking, planning, learning, working together. This is what we want for you; through guidance we will get there together.

School Characteristics:

Grade Levels: 6–8

Locale: Rural-remote

Total Students: 459

Male-Female Ratio: 53:47

Student-Teacher Ratio: 15.83:1

Free Lunch Eligible: 77.1%

Reduced-Price Lunch Eligible: 13.5%

Ethnicity	N	%
AmerInd/Alaskan	452	98.5
Asian	0	0.0
Black	1	0.2
Hispanic	0	0.0
White	6	1.3

General Information:

North U.S. Highway 163

Mustang Boulevard

Kayenta, AZ 86033

(928) 697-2303

www.kayentams.kayenta.k12.az.us/

Nay Ah Shing Schools
Onamia, Minnesota

Mission Statement

The mission of Nay Ah Shing School is to teach Ojibwe Language, Culture, Tradition, History, and Skills to live in 2 cultures by:

♦ Educating students academically, socially, emotionally, and physically in a safe and supportive environment.
♦ Building relationships and socializing skills by teaching respect for themselves, for Elders and for all individuals.
♦ Creating strong partnerships with parents.
♦ Accomodation of learning styles and teaching life skills.

School Characteristics:
Grade Levels: K–12
Locale: Rural[2]
Total Students: 154
Male-Female Ratio: N/A
Student-Teacher Ratio: 5.7:1
Free Lunch Eligible: N/A
Reduced-Price Lunch Eligible: N/A

Ethnicity	N	%
AmerInd/Alaskan	154	100.0
Asian	0	0.0
Black	0	0.0
Hispanic	0	0.0
White	0	0.0

General Information:
43651 Oodena Drive
Onamia, MN 56359
(320) 532-4695
www.nas.k12.mn.us/

[2]Locale not classified by CCD.

Nuweetooun School
Exeter, Rhode Island

Mission Statement

The mission of this school is to educate all students in a respectful, stimulating, and engaging environment. Our program integrates core educational curriculum standards in Language Arts, Mathematics, Science, Social Studies, and Health with a concentration on Environmental Education and Native Culture and History.

We are committed to creating an experiential, integrated, and collaborative learning environment in which to develop well-rounded, enthusiastic, and self-motivated learners. Our students experience education that embraces their learning styles, honors their multiple intelligences, and enriches their educational, social, spiritual, and cultural development in order to develop the whole person.

School Characteristics:

Grade Levels: K–8
Locale: Rural-remote
Total Students: 16
Male-Female Ratio: N/A
Student-Teacher Ratio: 8.0:1
Free Lunch Eligible: N/A
Reduced-Price Lunch Eligible: N/A

Ethnicity	N	%
AmerInd/Alaskan	16	100.0
Asian	0	0.0
Black	0	0.0
Hispanic	0	0.0
White	0	0.0

General Information:

390 Summit Rd
Exeter, RI 02822
(401) 491-9063
www.tomaquagmuseum.com/index.cfm?ac=school

10

Parochial Schools

Although parochial schools have traditionally referred to any school with a religious identity, the term today is nearly synonymous with Catholic schools or schools managed by and/or serving a local church diocese, community, or other private organization. Parochial schools are typically housed philosophically (and quite often geographically) within a Catholic church; however, they are often welcoming to children of all denominations and backgrounds.

Rather than receiving funds from the state and federal government, parochial schools are subsidized by donations and funds from their parishes and dioceses. In 2009, a study of American parochial high schools found the average annual tuition was $8,182, approximately 80 percent of actual per pupil cost of $10,228 (McDonald & Schultz, 2009). The same report stated that 97 percent of parochial high schools provided some form of tuition assistance to their students.

Parochial high schools generally emphasize a similar academic and college preparatory curriculum espoused by American public institutions, including sciences, mathematics, foreign languages, the arts, and the humanities. However, parochial schools have a strong emphasis on values-based education and a strong religious component rooted in the Old and New Testaments of the Bible as well as Catholic doctrine. Most parochial high schools also serve their community by providing students with catechetical training and instruction, whereby students prepare to officially join the congregation through the process of catechism/confirmation. In 2008, the US Conference of Catholic Bishops (USCCB) issued a curricular framework for the development of catechetical materials for "young people of high school age" (USCCB, 2008). The USCCB begins this curriculum framework stating that its program aims "to be a vehicle for growth in one's relationship with the Lord so that each may come to know him and live according to the truth he has given to us. In this way, disciples not only participate more deeply in the life of the Church but are also better able to reach eternal life with God in Heaven." (USCCB, 2008, p.1)

Today, more than 7,000 parochial schools enroll more than two million American children. Of these, 1,200 secondary schools serve approximately 600,000 high school students. The enrollment in parochial schools has decreased dramatically since the early 1960s, when more than 5 million American students attended 13,000 Catholic schools (McDonald & Schultz, 2009). Traditionally staffed by religious members and clergy, fewer than 5 percent of full-time teaching staff at Catholic high schools today are in the clergy.

Sources: McDonald & Schultz (2009); National Catholic Education Association (2010a); National Catholic Education Association (2010b); US Conference of Catholic Bishops (USCCB) (2008).

Archmere Academy
Claymont, Delaware

Mission Statement

Archmere Academy is a Roman Catholic, independent, college preparatory school inspired by the Norbertine tradition and a heritage of committed faculty, alumni, families, and friends. Archmere welcomes faculty and students of diverse religious and cultural backgrounds. Through dedication to academic excellence, social development, community service, and faith reflection, Archmere focuses on the education of the whole student. This philosophy encourages and supports the unique qualities and differences of students in achieving the maximum level of their abilities. Understanding their moral obligation to the global community, young men and women graduate from Archmere prepared for college, career and vocation in life.

School Characteristics:

Grade Levels: 9–12
Locale: Suburban-large
Total Students: 515
Male-Female Ratio: N/A
Student-Teacher Ratio: 9.5:1
Free Lunch Eligible: N/A
Reduced-Price Lunch Eligible: N/A

Ethnicity	N	%
AmerInd/Alaskan	0	0.0
Asian	0	0.0
Black	3	0.6
Hispanic	4	0.8
White	508	98.6

General Information:

3600 Philadelphia Pike
Claymont, DE 19703
(302) 798-6632
www.archmereacademy.com/

Brophy College Preparatory
Phoenix, Arizona

Mission Statement

Brophy is a private, Jesuit, Catholic, college preparatory that is committed to the belief that all creation is a reflection of God's love and presence which demands a passionate and generous response from the entire community. We are dedicated to students of all socio-economic backgrounds who have the potential and desire to maximize their God-given gifts. By creating an atmosphere for academic, emotional and spiritual growth, Brophy College Preparatory develops critically thinking, articulate, sensitive and aware students with a strong sense of self-worth. Through the process of nurturing the soul, Brophy offers these students an intimate relationship with God and inspires leaders who are devoted to the service of others in a global community.

School Characteristics:

Grade Levels: 9–12
Locale: City-large
Total Students: 1,270
Male-Female Ratio: 100:0
Student-Teacher Ratio: 12.2:1
Free Lunch Eligible: N/A
Reduced-Price Lunch Eligible: N/A

Ethnicity	N	%
AmerInd/Alaskan	6	0.5
Asian	62	4.9
Black	45	3.5
Hispanic	179	14.1
White	978	77.0

General Information:

4701 North Central Avenue
Phoenix, AZ 85012
(602) 264-5291
www.brophyprep.org/

Cardinal Newman School
Columbia, South Carolina

Mission Statement

With origins dating to 1858, Cardinal Newman School, a diocesan, coeducational, college preparatory secondary school serving grades 7 through 12, exists for the purpose of providing Catholic education of the highest quality to children of residents of the greater Columbia community. With an emphasis on the Catholic tradition of education—strong academics, a dedication to service, and traditional Catholic, Christian values, Cardinal Newman School provides a safe and structured environment which challenges all students to achieve personal excellence in every way. Inspired by the community belief in divine providence and love, Cardinal Newman students will become self-disciplined learners who also demonstrate respect, integrity, responsibility, and a sense of justice as they prepare to live lives of truth, integrity, and fidelity—**VERITAS, INTEGRITAS, FIDELITAS.**

School Characteristics:

Grade Levels: 7–12
Locale: Suburb-large
Total Students: 447
Male-Female Ratio: N/A
Student-Teacher Ratio: 10.8:1
Free Lunch Eligible: N/A
Reduced-Price Lunch Eligible: N/A

Ethnicity	N	%
AmerInd/Alaskan	0	0.0
Asian	9	2.0
Black	26	5.8
Hispanic	9	2.0
White	403	90.2

General Information:

4701 Forest Drive
Columbia, SC 29206
(803) 782-2814
www.cnhs.org/

Father Gabriel Richard Catholic High School
Ann Arbor, Michigan

Mission Statement

Father Gabriel Richard Regional Catholic High School is a regional, comprehensive, co-educational Catholic high school offering a value-centered education based upon Catholic principles and traditions. We are committed to providing the highest quality education to young men and women in a positive learning environment. We work cooperatively with parents in addressing individual needs and differences, fostering the students' spiritual, academic and physical development in preparing them to become faith-filled persons, lifelong learners and productive citizens.

School Characteristics:

Grade Levels: 9–12
Locale: Rural-fringe
Total Students: 501
Male-Female Ratio: N/A
Student-Teacher Ratio: N/A
Free Lunch Eligible: N/A
Reduced-Price Lunch Eligible: N/A

Ethnicity	N	%
AmerInd/Alaskan	2	0.4
Asian	8	1.6
Black	24	4.8
Hispanic	18	3.6
White	449	89.6

General Information:

4333 Whitehall Drive
Ann Arbor, MI 48105
(734) 662-0496
www.edline.net/pages/Fr_Gabriel_Richard_HS

Jesuit High School
Portland, Oregon

Mission Statement

Jesuit High School is a Catholic, college-preparatory school in the Jesuit tradition. It serves students of all religious faiths. Jesuit education fosters the harmonious development of the adolescent's gifts: spiritual, religious, intellectual, physical, emotional, and aesthetic. Jesuit High School hopes to accomplish this development by demonstrating a personal concern for individuals, a special concern for the poor, an articulate wisdom, enthusiasm, and a sense of community. In so doing, the school hopes to graduate leaders who are committed to serve God and their fellow men and women. Our hope is that our students develop a profound sense of justice founded in love, *i.e.*, leaders who are "men and women for others."

School Characteristics:

Grade Levels: 9–12
Locale: City-small
Total Students: 1,154
Male-Female Ratio: N/A
Student-Teacher Ratio: 15.5:1
Free Lunch Eligible: N/A
Reduced-Price Lunch Eligible: N/A

Ethnicity	N	%
AmerInd/Alaskan	1	0.1
Asian	89	7.7
Black	41	3.6
Hispanic	28	2.4
White	995	86.2

General Information:

9000 SW Beaverton-Hillsdale Highway
Portland, OR 97225
(503) 292-2663
www.jesuitportland.org/

Montgomery Catholic Preparatory School
Montgomery, Alabama

Mission Statement

Montgomery Catholic Preparatory School is an integral part of the Catholic Church's mission to proclaim the gospel of Jesus Christ. As an adult community, we share in the responsibility to prepare students for college and beyond while helping them grow to become persons of faith, virtue and wisdom.

School Characteristics:

Grade Levels: K–12
Locale: City-midsize
Total Students: 798
Male-Female Ratio: N/A
Student-Teacher Ratio: 13.7:1
Free Lunch Eligible: N/A
Reduced-Price Lunch Eligible: N/A

Ethnicity	N	%
AmerInd/Alaskan	0	0
Asian	15	1.8
Black	97	12.2
Hispanic	44	5.5
White	616	77.2

General Information:

5350 Vaughn Road
Montgomery, AL 36116
(334) 272-7220
www.knights.pvt.k12.al.us/highschool.cfm

Servite High School
Anaheim, California

Mission Statement

To provide a multifaceted and holistic educational experience which prepares students for post-secondary studies and responsible participation in the church and civic communities. To achieve excellence in a well-ordered and disciplined environment permeated by the Servite tradition of fraternity, service, and Marian spirituality. To assist each student in the full development of his gifts and talents through a challenging college preparatory academic program, athletic endeavors, and a well-rounded program of extra-curricular activities. To be a lived-faith community that awakens students and faculty to an inquiry into the meaning of their spiritual lives through religious studies, shared worship, campus ministry, and Christian Service programs. To respect the dignity and rights of all fculty and student body membrs and in accord with the collegial tradition of the Order of Friar Servants of Mary.

School Characteristics:

Grade Levels: 9–12
Locale: City-large
Total Students: 881
Male-Female Ratio: N/A
Student-Teacher Ratio: 13.5:1
Free Lunch Eligible: N/A
Reduced-Price Lunch Eligible: N/A

General Information:

1952 West La Palma Avenue
Anaheim, CA 92801
(714) 774-7575
http://servitehs.org/

Student population data not available from the CCD or Greatschools.net.

St. Mary's High School
St. Louis, Missouri

Mission Statement

◆ To help each young man discover that life as a Christian is a journey that must be rooted in God

◆ To develop in the young man a deep sense of the goodness, self-worth and the dignity of every person

◆ To maintain a community where all involved in the students' formation collaborate to create a climate of cooperation, respect, openness and trust

◆ To provide a comprehensive program of learning which challenges and motivates each student to reach his fullest potential

◆ To instruct each young man in the Marianist spirit

School Characteristics:

Grade Levels: 9–12
Locale: City-large
Total Students: 409
Male-Female Ratio: 100:0
Student-Teacher Ratio: 12.7:1
Free Lunch Eligible: N/A
Reduced-Price Lunch Eligible: N/A

Ethnicity	N	%
AmerInd/Alaskan	2	0.5
Asian	9	2.2
Black	19	4.6
Hispanic	10	2.4
White	369	90.2

General Information:

4701 South Grand
St. Louis, MO 63111
(314) 481-8400
www.stmaryshs.com/

Totino-Grace High School
Fridley, Minnesota

Mission Statement

Totino-Grace is an Archdiocesan co-educational Catholic high school in the Lasallian tradition. Welcoming a student body that is academically, economically, and culturally diverse, we strive for equity and excellence in all programs. Recognizing the key elements of our mission as learning, faith, community, and service, we seek to provide a safe environment that places priority on mutual respect, self-discipline, and acknowledgment of our responsibility in the world community.

School Characteristics:

Grade Levels: 9–12
Locale: Suburb-large
Total Students: 1,015
Male-Female Ratio: N/A
Student-Teacher Ratio: 15.6:1
Free Lunch Eligible: N/A
Reduced-Price Lunch Eligible: N/A

Ethnicity	N	%
AmerInd/Alaskan	11	1.1
Asian	37	3.6
Black	32	3.2
Hispanic	27	2.7
White	908	89.5

General Information:

1350 Gardena Avenue NE
Fridley, MN 55432
(763) 571-9116
www.totinograce.org/

11

Waldorf Schools

Nearly a hundred years ago, a prominent social reformer asked Rudolf Steiner (1861–1925) to design a new school for the children of workers at the Waldorf-Astoria Cigarette Factory in Stuttgart, Germany. At the time Steiner was asked to design and build this new "Waldorf" school in 1919, he was already prominent as a cultural philosopher, author, lecturer, and spiritualist.

Since their inception, Waldorf Schools have emphasized a holistic approach to education founded on the educational and developmental theories of Rudolf Steiner. Waldorf schools are officially non-denominational and non-sectarian but seek to include a wider educational, social, emotional and spiritual focus than is traditionally offered in American public schools. Indeed, Waldorf schools purport to develop the whole child.

In early education, schools often emphasize handwork, storytelling, cooking, painting, nature time, and free play, while providing relatively little direct instruction and focus on traditional academic and cognitive subject areas. As a student progresses through later grades (often continuing or looping with the same teacher for multiple years), the focus remains on the "whole child" with direct participation required in music, dance, theater, as well as writing, literature, foreign languages, world history, observational sciences, and mathematics.

Today, there are nearly 1,000 Waldorf schools around the world. In the US, the first Waldorf school opened in 1928, and currently, approximately 200 Waldorf elementary, middle, and high schools are operating across the country, of which at least thirty are publicly funded through public school systems. Waldorf schools have experienced much growth in the last generation, as evidenced by the doubling of Waldorf high schools in North America over the past ten years.

Sources: Association of Waldorf Schools of North America (n.d.); Waldorf School Association (n.d.); Word List of Rudolf Steiner (Waldorf) Schools and Teacher Training Centers (2011).

Academe of the Oaks
Decatur, Georgia

Mission Statement

Adolescents today are inheriting a world with staggering challenges. To meet those challenges and solve ever more complex problems, our young men and women will need a strong sense of moral and ethical responsibility, tremendous creativity, inner strength, and the ability to work with each other in a global context.

At Academe of the Oaks, our mission is to re-define the high school experience by educating our students to be resourceful, clear, and flexible thinkers, capable of making profound and positive contributions to the fast-changing world they inherit.

School Characteristics:

Grade Levels: 9–12
Locale: Large Suburb
Total Students: 34
Male-Female Ratio: N/A
Student-Teacher Ratio: 5.0:1
Free Lunch Eligible: N/A
Reduced-Price Lunch Eligible: N/A

Ethnicity	N	%
AmerInd/Alaskan	0	0.0
Asian	0	0.0
Black	7	20.6
Hispanic	0	0.0
White	27	79.4

General Information:

146 New Street
Decatur, GA 30030
(404) 405-2173
www.academeatlanta.org/

Desert Marigold School
Phoenix, Arizona

Mission Statement

Inspired by Rudolf Steiner's Waldorf Education system, the mission of Desert Marigold School is to provide an educational context that emphasizes not only intellectual achievement, but also the imaginative, artistic, and moral growth of its students. By addressing their heads, hands and hearts, the school will encourage students to be life-long learners and independent thinkers as well as self-motivated, self-disciplined, creative, adaptable and responsible individuals.

We seek to establish and maintain a school that provides an individualized, nurturing approach to educating its students, preparing them not only for higher education, but for the rest of their lives. We will require and use an active partnership of teachers, families and the community, as well as a continued affiliation with the world-wide Waldorf movement to achieve the following goals:

1. To ensure each child's excellence in core academic skills by providing a curriculum enlivened with the arts of painting, music, drama, movement, singing, sculpture and hand work.
2. To educate according to age and development, so that learning and growth are united.
3. To present the curriculum in multiple and integrated ways, so students have many different opportunities to learn concepts, as well as see the relationship to the larger whole.
4. To nourish the spirit of curiosity so that students continue to learn long after the end of formal training.
5. To encourage fundamental values and life skills, including responsibility, perseverance, integrity, self-discipline, trustworthiness, craftsmanship, friendship and compassion.
6. To make available this quality of education for all ethnic and socio-economic sectors in our community.

School Characteristics:

Grade Levels: K–9

Locale: City-large

Total Students: 198

Male-Female Ratio: 52:48

Student-Teacher Ratio: N/A

Free Lunch Eligible: 10.1%

Reduced-Price Lunch Eligible: 4.0%

Ethnicity	N	%
AmerInd/Alaskan	6	3.0
Asian	14	7.1
Black	10	5.1
Hispanic	17	8.6
White	151	76.3

General Information:

6210 South 28th Street

Phoenix, AZ 85042

(602) 243-6909

http://arizonawaldorf.org/DMS/

Emerson Waldorf School
Chapel Hill, North Carolina

Mission Statement

Emerson Waldorf School provides an integrated Waldorf curriculum and environment which encourage and promote independent thinking and social responsibility, as well as academic and artistic excellence. The unique gifts and contributions of each child are honored through a developmentally appropriate awakening of thinking, feeling and willing.

Further, the Emerson Waldorf School understands children as beings of body, soul and spirit, and guides them to develop compassion and reverence for themselves and the world community.

School Characteristics:
Grade Levels: PreK–12
Locale: Rural-fringe
Total Students: 255
Male-Female Ratio: N/A
Student-Teacher Ratio: 8.6:1
Free Lunch Eligible: N/A
Reduced-Price Lunch Eligible: N/A

Ethnicity	N	%
AmerInd/Alaskan	0	0.0
Asian	8	3.3
Black	5	2.1
Hispanic	2	0.8
White	224	93.7

General Information:
6211 New Jericho Road
Chapel Hill, NC 27516
(919) 967-1858
www.emersonwaldorf.org/

Honolulu Waldorf School
Honolulu, Hawaii

Mission Statement

Honolulu Waldorf School provides an education that fosters in each child a sense of meaning and purpose in life, and the confidence to meet his or her individual destiny.

We recognize and welcome the unique gifts brought by each child we serve. We are committed to supporting each child in his or her intellectual, physical, emotional, and spiritual development by offering a will-based curriculum that integrates academic, practical, experiential, and artistic work. We educate each child so that he or she will contribute to the future of the world with clear and creative thinking, compassion and moral strength, and the courage to initiate change.

We are inspired and guided in our work by the educational and spiritual insights of Rudolf Steiner and the continually growing body of research in anthroposphy, which maintains that the highest goal of education is the realization of responsible human freedom.

School Characteristics:

Grade Levels: PreK–12
Locale: City-large
Total Students: 313
Male-Female Ratio: N/A
Student-Teacher Ratio: N/A
Free Lunch Eligible: N/A
Reduced-Price Lunch Eligible: N/A

Ethnicity	N	%
AmerInd/Alaskan	3	1.2
Asian	89	34.6
Black	11	4.3
Hispanic	14	5.4
White	140	54.5

General Information:

350 Ulua Street
Honolulu, HI 96821
(808) 377-5471
www.honoluluwaldorf.org/

The Bay School
Blue Hill, Maine

Mission Statement

The Bay School's mission is to provide an education that engages and nurtures the whole child, inspiring a balanced growth of heart, mind body and spirit. We are committed to developing in our students inner confidence, responsibility, self-motivation, a love of learning, imagination, creativity and intellectual clarity. The educational ideals and values of the school, rooted in the Waldorf tradition, create a community of children, alumni, parents and faculty imbued with reverence for others and the natural world.

School Characteristics:
Grade Levels: PreK–8
Locale: Rural-remote
Total Students: 94
Male-Female Ratio: N/A
Student-Teacher Ratio: 9.7:1
Free Lunch Eligible: N/A
Reduced-Price Lunch Eligible: N/A

Ethnicity	N	%
AmerInd/Alaskan	0	0.0
Asian	4	4.5
Black	0	0.0
Hispanic	0	0.0
White	84	95.5

General Information:
P.O. Box 950, South Street
Blue Hill, ME 04614
(207) 374-2187
www.bayschool.org/

Waldorf School of Princeton
Princeton, New Jersey

Mission Statement

The Waldorf School of Princeton, part of an independent educational movement of over 1,000 schools worldwide, is dedicated to recognizing the unique spirit of each child. Through a rich curriculum integrating the academic, the artistic, and the practical, the Waldorf School of Princeton guides children toward self-knowledge, to meet the world by awakening within them warmth of heart, clarity of thought, and strength of purpose.

School Characteristics:

Grade Levels: PreK–8
Locale: Suburb-large
Total Students: 177
Male-Female Ratio: N/A
Student-Teacher Ratio: N/A
Free Lunch Eligible: N/A
Reduced-Price Lunch Eligible: N/A

Ethnicity	N	%
AmerInd/Alaskan	0	0.0
Asian	14	11.1
Black	7	5.5
Hispanic	1	0.8
White	104	85.5

General Information:

1062 Cherry Hill Rd
Princeton, NJ 08540
(609) 466-1970
www.princetonwaldorf.org/histphil.html

Waldorf School on the Roaring Fork
Carbondale, Colorado

Mission Statement

Inspiring the spirit of the child through educational artistry and academic rigor.

School Characteristics:

Grade Levels: PreK–8
Locale: Rural-fringe
Total Students: 187
Male-Female Ratio: N/A
Student-Teacher Ratio: 10.6:1
Free Lunch Eligible: N/A
Reduced-Price Lunch Eligible: N/A

Ethnicity	N	%
AmerInd/Alaskan	0	0.0
Asian	4	2.3
Black	0	0.0
Hispanic	3	1.7
White	167	96.0

General Information:

16543 Highway 82
Carbondale, CO 81623
(970) 963-1960
www.waldorfcarbondale.org/

12

Montessori Schools

More than a century ago, Italian born physician Maria Montessori (1870–1952) founded her first experimental preschool in a low-income Rome neighborhood. Using a research-based approach that focused on observation of students engaged in free play, Montessori developed educational materials and methods that facilitated and replicated children's natural inquiry and self-direction. Initially working with special needs populations, Montessori built on her discoveries that children can teach themselves, which led to strong performance gains on state-level reading and writing exams. These approaches and their subsequent results led to one of the world's most famous educational movements of the 20th century.

Since their inception, Montessori schools have emphasized a holistic and nurturing approach to education founded on the educational and developmental theories of Maria Montessori. Curricular subjects are typically interwoven, rather than taught independently, and students work independently or in small groups, often in classrooms with multiage students. Traditionally, formalized assessments and grades are not employed, while teachers emphasize self-paced learning and hands-on activities to encourage children's natural curiosity, inquiry, and exploration.

Today, approximately 8,000 Montessori schools can be found around the world. In the US, the first Montessori schools opened nearly a century ago, although nearly all the nation's 4,000 Montessori schools were founded since the 1960s. Though the majority of American Montessori schools are private and focus on early and elementary education, a growing number schools (currently about 300) are publicly funded through traditional school systems. Although some have religious affiliations, the majority of Montessori schools in the US operate independently.

Sources: Dohrmann, Nishida, Gartner, Lipsky, & Grimm (2007); Montessori Foundation (2011).

Austin Montessori School
Austin, Texas

Mission Statement

The mission of Austin Montessori School is to guide the intellectual and character development of each child along a path towards his full and unknown potential. We strive to cultivate compassion and respect, independence and belonging, and freedom and self-discipline, in rich academic and social environments that are designed for each plane of development and honor the complementary needs of the individual and the group. We value an educational setting that is inclusive and recognizes the authentic nature of the child and nurtures a reverence for the organic order of the universe. Through parent and staff education, we work to develop a school and family culture that preserves and protects a healthy childhood. Our aim is to serve children possessing an ample range of temperaments and a variety of learning styles and rates. At the same time we seek to avoid pathologizing and labeling the normal range of children's behaviors and differences in learning. We are dedicated to Montessori's mission of world peace through human development.

School Characteristics:
Grade Levels: PreK–9
Locale: City-large
Total Students: 218
Male-Female Ratio: N/A
Student-Teacher Ratio: 15.6:1
Free Lunch Eligible: N/A
Reduced-Price Lunch Eligible: N/A

Ethnicity	N	%
AmerInd/Alaskan	0	0.0
Asian	23	10.6
Black	0	0.0
Hispanic	15	6.9
White	180	82.6

General Information:
506 Sunset Trail
Austin, TX 78745
(512) 892-0253
www.austinmontessori.org

Casa Dei Bambini
Marietta, Georgia

Mission Statement

Casa's mission is to motivate its students from within by a natural curiosity and love for knowledge. The goal of education should not be to fill the child with facts but rather to cultivate his/her own natural desire to learn.

School Characteristics:
Grade Levels: "Ungraded"
Locale: City-small
Total Students: 162
Male-Female Ratio: N/A
Student-Teacher Ratio: 23.1:1
Free Lunch Eligible: N/A
Reduced-Price Lunch Eligible: N/A

General Information:
150 Powers Ferry Road
Marietta, GA 30067
(770) 973-2731
www.casamontessori.com/

Student population data not available from the CCD or Greatschools.net.

Chesterfield Montessori School
Chesterfield, Missouri

Mission Statement

Chesterfield Montessori School offers an authentic Montessori education that honors children's individuality. Our peaceful environment and compassionate staff nurtures respect for self and others, fosters a strong sense of community, and stimulates independent thinking. Students carry with them a solid record of academic achievement, a belief in the dignity of work, and a sense of responsibility for their own development as happy and productive human beings.

School Characteristics:

Grade Levels: PreK–6
Locale: Suburb-large
Total Students: 86
Male-Female Ratio: N/A
Student-Teacher Ratio: 12.36:1
Free Lunch Eligible: N/A
Reduced-Price Lunch Eligible: N/A

Ethnicity	N	%
AmerInd/Alaskan	0	0.0
Asian	17	19.8
Black	9	10.5
Hispanic	1	1.2
White	59	68.6

General Information:

14000 Ladue Road
Chesterfield, MO 63017
(314) 469-7150
www.cmsstl.org

Dynamite Montessori
Cave Creek, Arizona

Mission Statement

Dynamite Montessori is a joyful place where children's spontaneity is expressed, where community is fostered, and respect is practiced. It is a safe place where the wonders of nature are discovered, and people experience kindness as the powerful force it is. Ours is a place where bilingual education is pursued, strong bodies are nurtured, lifelong friendships are formed, and the love of learning never wanes.

School Characteristics:
Grade Levels: PreK–4
Locale: Suburb-large
Total Students: 134
Male-Female Ratio: N/A
Student-Teacher Ratio: 8.7:1
Free Lunch Eligible: N/A
Reduced-Price Lunch Eligible: N/A

General Information:
28807 North 53rd Street
Cave Creek, AZ 85331
(480) 563-5710
www.dynamitemontessori.com/

Student population data not available from the CCD or Greatschools.net.

Montessori School at Holy Rosary
Cleveland, Ohio

Mission Statement

The Montessori School at Holy Rosary is dedicated to providing outstanding educational instruction by discovering and awakening children's emerging potential and carefully cultivating the development of their innate talents and abilities.

We are vitally committed to providing excellence in education to the children of Greater Cleveland through the philosophy and techniques of the Montessori method, provided in a Catholic atmosphere, enriched by the values of love, respect, and justice. The Montessori School at Holy Rosary is established to serve all children, regardless of race or creed, and is uniquely devoted to enhancing the vitality of Holy Rosary Parish and the Little Italy community.

School Characteristics:
Grade Levels: PreK–8
Locale: City-large
Total Students: 105
Male-Female Ratio: N/A
Student-Teacher Ratio: 14.3:1
Free Lunch Eligible: N/A
Reduced-Price Lunch Eligible: N/A

Ethnicity	N	%
AmerInd/Alaskan	0	0.0
Asian	7	11.1
Black	8	12.7
Hispanic	2	3.2
White	46	73.0

General Information:
12009 Mayfield Road
Cleveland, OH 44106
(216) 421-0700
www.montessori-holyrosary.org/

Pacific Rim International School
Emeryville, California

Mission Statement

Pacific Rim International School (PRINTS) strives to nurture in children bilingualism and internationalism in an AMI Montessori environment.

School Characteristics:

Grade Levels: K–1
Locale: Suburb-large
Total Students: 13
Male-Female Ratio: N/A
Student-Teacher Ratio: 2.6:1
Free Lunch Eligible: N/A
Reduced-Price Lunch Eligible: N/A

Ethnicity	N	%
AmerInd/Alaskan	0	0.0
Asian	5	38.5
Black	0	0.0
Hispanic	0	0.0
White	2	15.4
Two or more races	6	46.2

General Information:

5521 Doyle Street
Emeryville, CA 94608
(510) 601-1500
www.pacificriminternationalschool.org/

The Cobb School Montessori
Simsbury, Connecticut

Mission Statement

Believe, Guide, Step Aside, Let Fly.

School Characteristics:

Grade Levels: PreK–6
Locale: Suburb-large
Total Students: 89
Male-Female Ratio: N/A
Student-Teacher Ratio: 13.1:1
Free Lunch Eligible: N/A
Reduced-Price Lunch Eligible: N/A

Ethnicity	N	%
AmerInd/Alaskan	0	0.0
Asian	1	1.1
Black	0	0.0
Hispanic	1	1.1
White	89	97.8

General Information:

112 Sand Hill Road
Simsbury, CT 06070
(860) 658-1144
www.cobbschool.com/

13

Apple Computer Schools of Distinction

In the past few decades, the widespread adoption and use of computer technologies has transformed nearly all facets of American life. Education has also been markedly changed as computer-based technologies and digital tools have become incorporated into various levels of the school system. Today, nearly all US classrooms have Internet connectivity, and one school computer is available for every four students in public schools (Bebell & Kay, 2010). Many schools, districts, and states have pushed the technology envelop further by providing one to one student access to individual computers, and many state programs allow students to take their school laptops home, as was previously required for papers, textbooks, and homework. Like the majority of today's population, students of all demographic backgrounds across the country now overwhelmingly report widespread access to and use of computers in their homes for a wide variety of purposes.

The Apple Schools of Distinction and the Distinguished Educator (ADE) programs are award programs focused on recognizing educational excellence and leadership in both K–12 and higher education settings. Awardees are distinguished for their identified expertise on educational technology leadership and include more than 1,500 educators and schools across the globe. In this chapter, we share examples of schools that have been recognized as advocates and innovators of educational technology and represent some of the leading perspectives in the use of educational technology to improve teaching and learning.

Del Mar Middle School
Tiburon, California

Mission Statement

Together we provide our children with extraordinary opportunities to enlighten their minds, inspire their hearts and strengthen their resolve to positively impact their world.

School Characteristics:

Grade Levels: 6–8
Locale: Suburb-large
Total Students: 359
Male-Female Ratio: 54:46
Student-Teacher Ratio: 14.2:1
Free Lunch Eligible: 0%
Reduced-Price Lunch Eligible: 0%

Ethnicity	N	%
AmerInd/Alaskan	0	0.0
Asian	33	9.2
Black	4	1.1
Hispanic	18	5.0
White	295	82.2
Two or more races	9	2.5

General Information:

105 Avenida Miraflores
Tiburon, CA 94920
(415) 435-1468
http://delmar.reedschools.org/

Echo Lake Elementary School
Shoreline, Washington

Mission Statement

The mission of the Shoreline School District is to provide a collaborative learning community which engages all students in learning the academic and work-life skills needed to achieve their individual potential and become responsible citizens.

School Characteristics:

Grade Levels: K–6
Locale: Suburb-large
Total Students: 447
Male-Female Ratio: 53:47
Student-Teacher Ratio: 18.2:1
Free Lunch Eligible: 24.1%
Reduced-Price Lunch Eligible: 9.6%

Ethnicity	N	%
AmerInd/Alaskan	4	1.0
Asian	122	29.6
Black	42	10.2
Hispanic	46	11.2
White	202	49.0

General Information:

19345 Wallingford North
Shoreline, WA 98133
(206) 393-4338
www.shorelineschools.org/schools/profiles/echo_lake.php

Empire High School
Tucson, Arizona

Mission Statement

It is the mission of Empire High School for students to become self-directed learners through positive relationships. Empire is . . . Culture-rich, Innovative, Challenging.

School Characteristics:

Grade Levels: 9–12
Locale: Rural-fringe
Total Students: 792
Male-Female Ratio: 53:47
Student-Teacher Ratio: 16.3:1
Free Lunch Eligible: 8.1%
Reduced-Price Lunch Eligible: 3.8%

Ethnicity	N	%
AmerInd/Alaskan	4	0.5
Asian	27	3.5
Black	31	4.0
Hispanic	137	17.5
White	583	74.6

General Information:

10701 East Mary Ann Cleveland Way
Tucson, AZ 85747
(520) 879-3000
http://ehs.vail.k12.az.us

Howard Elementary School
Eugene, Oregon

Mission Statement

We seek to maintain a spirit of joy in learning, cooperation in doing, and optimism for success and the future. Our goal is to have every student exceed state standards in all academic areas.

School Characteristics:

Grade Levels: K–5

Locale: City-midsize

Total Students: 312

Male-Female Ratio: 43:57

Student-Teacher Ratio: 19.3:1

Free Lunch Eligible: 58.3%

Reduced-Price Lunch Eligible: 11.5%

Ethnicity	N	%
AmerInd/Alaskan	5	1.8
Asian	5	1.8
Black	2	0.7
Hispanic	68	24.3
White	200	71.4

General Information:

700 Howard Ave

Eugene, OR 97404

(541) 790-4900

www.howardelementary.org/school/profile/

Lilla G. Frederick Pilot Middle School
Dorchester, Massachusetts

Mission Statement

To provide students in grades six through eight with a rigorous academic curriculum within a stimulating and nurturing environment. The school serves the whole child—mind, body and spirit—as well as families and the community in which the children reside. Inquiry, exploration, experience, connections and hands-on learning all facilitate and complement the core academic curricula and support the school's vision of developing life-long learners.

School Characteristics:

Grade Levels: 6–8
Locale: City-large
Total Students: 640
Male-Female Ratio: 53:47
Student-Teacher Ratio: 11.9:1
Free Lunch Eligible: 80.3%
Reduced-Price Lunch Eligible: 5.6%

Ethnicity	N	%
AmerInd/Alaskan	1	0.2
Asian	7	1.1
Black	337	52.7
Hispanic	265	41.4
White	24	3.8
Two or more races	6	0.9

General Information:

270 Columbia Road
Dorchester, MA 02121
(617) 635-1650
www.lgfnet.org/

Science Leadership Academy
Philadelphia, Pennsylvania

Mission Statement

"How do we learn?" "What can we create?" "What does it mean to lead?" These three essential questions form the basis of instruction at the Science Leadership Academy (SLA), a Philadelphia high school opened in September 2006. SLA is built on the notion that inquiry is the very first step in the process of learning. Developed in partnership with The Franklin Institute and its commitment to inquiry-based science, SLA provides a rigorous, college-preparatory curriculum with a focus on science, technology, mathematics and entrepreneurship. Students at SLA learn in a project-based environment where the core values of inquiry, research, collaboration, presentation and reflection are emphasized in all classes. The structure of the Science Leadership Academy reflects its core values, with longer class periods to allow for more laboratory work in science classes and performance-based learning in all classes. In addition, students in the upper grades have more flexible schedules to allow for opportunities for dual enrollment programs with area universities and career development internships in laboratory and business settings, as well as with The Franklin Institute. At SLA, learning is not just something that happens from 8:30am to 3:00pm, but a continuous process that expands beyond the four walls of the classroom into every facet of our lives.

School Characteristics:

Grade Levels: 9–12
Locale: City-large
Total Students: 336
Male-Female Ratio: 47:53
Student-Teacher Ratio: 2.0:1
Free Lunch Eligible: 19.4%
Reduced-Price Lunch Eligible: 3.0%

Ethnicity	N	%
AmerInd/Alaskan	0	0.0
Asian	26	7.1
Black	186	51.1
Hispanic	24	6.6
White	128	35.2

General Information:

2130 Arch St.
Philadelphia, PA 19103
(215) 979-5620
www.scienceleadership.org/

The Urban School of San Francisco
San Francisco, California

Mission Statement

The Urban School of San Francisco seeks to ignite a passion for learning, inspiring its students to become self-motivated, enthusiastic participants in their education—both in high school and beyond.

School Characteristics:

Grade Levels: 9–12
Locale: City-large
Total Students: 342
Male-Female Ratio: N/A
Student-Teacher Ratio: 9.8:1
Free Lunch Eligible: N/A
Reduced-Price Lunch Eligible: N/A

Ethnicity	N	%
AmerInd/Alaskan	0	0
Asian	35	10.2
Black	13	3.8
Hispanic	8	2.3
White	286	83.6

General Information:

1563 Page Street
San Francisco, CA 94117
(415) 626-2919
www.urbanschool.org/

Washington Middle School
Kenosha, Wisconsin

Mission Statement

To empower all students to become motivated independent thinkers prepared to excel at the next level, by creating an environment that provides a quality education which integrates technology, expects family involvement, and implements research-based instruction. We believe that laptop learning engages our students in more dynamic ways, allowing them to explore world-wide information sources, enhance academic and fine arts skills, and organize their work more effectively. We are developing 21st Century learners.

School Characteristics:

Grade Levels: 6–8
Locale: Suburb-midsize
Total Students: 621
Male-Female Ratio: 50:50
Student-Teacher Ratio: 14.7:1
Free Lunch Eligible: 50.4%
Reduced-Price Lunch Eligible: 9.7%

Ethnicity	N	%
AmerInd/Alaskan	1	0.2
Asian	7	1.1
Black	144	23.2
Hispanic	178	28.7
White	291	46.9

General Information:

811 Washington Rd
Kenosha, WI 53140
(262) 359-6291
http://washington.kusd.edu/

Westside High School
Omaha, Nebraska

Mission Statement

In its quest to be the best high school in the United States and achieve unequaled excellence, Westside's Mission is to ensure that all students reach for their potential, compete successfully in a changing world, and demonstrate respect for themselves, others, and their environment.

School Characteristics:

Grade Levels: 9–12
Locale: City-large
Total Students: 1,993
Male-Female Ratio: 54:46
Student-Teacher Ratio: 14.8:1
Free Lunch Eligible: 10.5%
Reduced-Price Lunch Eligible: 6.0%

Ethnicity	N	%
AmerInd/Alaskan	22	1.1
Asian	71	3.6
Black	133	6.7
Hispanic	79	4.0
White	1,688	84.7

General Information:

8701 Pacific Street
Omaha, NE 68114
(402) 343-2600
http://whs.westside66.org/

14

Award Winning Schools

A variety of award programs across the country have been set up to recognize schools with a commitment to excellence. Different criteria are used to judge school quality, but the most comprehensive of these programs is the US Department of Education's Blue Ribbon Schools Program (www2.ed.gov/programs/nclbbrs/index.html). Initiated in 1982, the Blue Ribbon Schools program identifies public and private elementary, middle, and high schools whose students achieve at very high levels on state tests or who have made significant gains in student achievement over a five-year period. There is also an emphasis on recognizing schools serving disadvantaged and minority students. According to the Department of Education, just 6,000 schools out of a possible 138,000 schools (4.3 percent) have received this award over the past twenty-eight years. One of the key criteria in the selection process is that Blue Ribbon school leaders articulate a vision of excellence for their school. Public schools are nominated by the Chief State School Officers (CCSOs) and by officials at the Department of Defense Education Academy (DoDEA) and the Bureau of Indian Education (BIE). Private schools are nominated by the Council for American Private Education (CAPE). The purpose of the program is to recognize those schools whose students have thrived and excelled, sometimes against the odds.

Another award program that has risen to prominence in recent years is *Newsweek* Magazine's list of America's Best High Schools. According to *Newsweek*, a total of 1,600 schools (6 percent of all public schools) made the list in 2010 (www.newsweek.com/feature/2010/americas-best-high-schools.html). *Newsweek*'s primary criterion for selection is the number of advance placement courses offered by the schools and the students' level of achievement on state tests.

Sources: The Daily Beast (2010); US Department of Education (2011a).

BASIS Tucson
Tucson, Arizona

Mission Statement

BASIS seeks to raise academic expectations to internationally competitive levels for all students. By offering an academically excellent and rigorous liberal arts college preparatory education, BASIS prepares students to compete for admissions and scholarships to top colleges and universities.

School Characteristics:

Grade Levels: 5–12
Locale: City-large
Total Students: 558
Male-Female Ratio: 51:49
Student-Teacher Ratio: N/A
Free Lunch Eligible: N/A
Reduced-Price Lunch Eligible: N/A

Ethnicity	N	%
AmerInd/Alaskan	14	2.2
Asian	121	18.6
Black	26	4.0
Hispanic	134	20.6
White	356	54.7

General Information:

3434 East Broadway Boulevard
Tucson, AZ 85716
(520) 326-3444
www.basistucson.org/
Newsweek's Best High Schools (2010)

Chapin High School
Chapin, South Carolina

Mission Statement

The mission of Chapin High School of Lexington Richland School District Five, in partnership with the community, is to provide challenging curricula with high expectations for learning that develop productive citizens who can solve problems and contribute to a global society.

School Characteristics:

Grade Levels: 9–12
Locale: Rural-fringe
Total Students: 1,248
Male-Female Ratio: 52:48
Student-Teacher Ratio: 13.8:1
Free Lunch Eligible: 7.5%
Reduced-Price Lunch Eligible: 2.0%

Ethnicity	N	%
AmerInd/Alaskan	2	0.2
Asian	21	1.7
Black	59	4.7
Hispanic	22	1.8
White	1,141	91.6

General Information:

300 Columbia Avenue
Chapin, SC 29036
(803) 575-5400
www.lex5.k12.sc.us/ChapinHS.cfm
*US DOE Blue Ribbon School

Columbiana High School
Columbiana, Ohio

Mission Statement

The mission of Columbiana High School and the community at large is to educate all students to achieve their highest individual academic potential, as well as cultivate a sense of personal integrity.

School Characteristics:

Grade Levels: 9–12
Locale: Town-fringe
Total Students: 338
Male-Female Ratio: 50:50
Student-Teacher Ratio: 17.0:1
Free Lunch Eligible: 25.7%
Reduced-Price Lunch Eligible: 10.4%

Ethnicity	N	%
AmerInd/Alaskan	0	0.0
Asian	3	0.9
Black	4	1.2
Hispanic	8	2.4
White	318	95.5

General Information:

700 Columbiana-Waterford Road
Columbiana, OH 44408
(330) 482-3818
www.columbiana.k12.oh.us/HighSchool/
*US DOE Blue Ribbon School

Devine High School
Devine, Texas

Mission Statement

The staff of Devine High School believes that each student has the ability to learn. In order for each student to achieve his or her goals in academic and/or vocational development, our mission will be to meet student needs at all levels, motivating and encouraging each student regardless of his or her academic level, socioeconomic status, race, or gender. Upon completion of our mission, each student should be able to make a smooth transition to college, trade or vocational school, military service, or the workplace.

School Characteristics:

Grade Levels: 9–12
Locale: Town-remote
Total Students: 533
Male-Female Ratio: 52:48
Student-Teacher Ratio: 12.8:1
Free Lunch Eligible: 29.1%
Reduced-Price Lunch Eligible: 10.1%

Ethnicity	N	%
AmerInd/Alaskan	2	0.4
Asian	1	0.2
Black	5	0.9
Hispanic	274	51.4
White	251	47.1

General Information:

1225 W Highway 173
Devine, TX 78016
(830) 851-0895
www.devineisd.org/highschool/
*US DOE Blue Ribbon School

Eastside High School
Gainesville, Florida

Mission Statement

Eastside High School seeks to build community among our highly diverse students and their families, whether they come from different neighborhoods in Gainesville or from countries and cultures around the world. All members of our fluid and lively school family—parents, students, faculty, and support staff—should show respect and encouragement for each other. The mission of Eastside High School's community is that all students develop the skills and knowledge necessary for them to survive, learn, adapt, and grow—leading to a lifetime pattern of responsible citizenship.

School Characteristics:

Grade Levels: 9–12
Locale: Suburban-midsize
Total Students: 1,741
Male-Female Ratio: 45:55
Student-Teacher Ratio: 15.5:1
Free Lunch Eligible: 36.0%
Reduced-Price Lunch Eligible: 5.7%

Ethnicity	N	%
AmerInd/Alaskan	2	0.1
Asian	47	3.0
Black	1,019	64.2
Hispanic	54	3.4
White	466	29.3

General Information:

1201 SE 43rd Street
Gainesville, FL 32641
(352) 955-6704
www.sbac.edu/~ehs/
Newsweek's Best High Schools (2010)

Hingham High School
Hingham, Massachusetts

Mission Statement

The mission of Hingham High School is to graduate students with the academic, civic, social, and personal skills necessary to become productive, responsible members of a democratic and ever-changing global society. With the support and involvement of the community, Hingham High School will engage all students in a challenging, well-balanced educational program complemented by co-curricular activities.

School Characteristics:

Grade Levels: 9–12
Locale: Surburb-large
Total Students: 1,038
Male-Female Ratio: 51:49
Student-Teacher Ratio: 13.2:1
Free Lunch Eligible: 1.9%
Reduced-Price Lunch Eligible: 1.2%

Ethnicity	N	%
AmerInd/Alaskan	0	0.0
Asian	19	1.8
Black	19	1.8
Hispanic	29	2.8
White	941	90.7
Two or more races	30	2.9

General Information:

17 Union Street
Hingham, MA 02043
(781)741-1560
http://hinghamschools.com/index.asp?site=1
*US DOE Blue Ribbon School

Lakeville North High School
Lakeville, Minnesota

Mission Statement

Lakeville North High School is committed to creating a community that instills integrity and challenges students to reach their individual potential.

School Characteristics:

Grade Levels: 9–12
Locale: Suburb-large
Total Students: 1,761
Male-Female Ratio: 53:47
Student-Teacher Ratio: 20.1:1
Free Lunch Eligible: 3.5%
Reduced-Price Lunch Eligible: 1.5%

Ethnicity	N	%
AmerInd/Alaskan	3	0.2
Asian	69	3.9
Black	65	3.7
Hispanic	51	2.9
White	1,573	89.3

General Information:

19600 Ipava Avenue West
Lakeville, MN 55044
(952) 232-3600
www.lnhs.isd194.k12.mn.us/
*US DOE Blue Ribbon School

Leo Junior/Senior High School
Leo, Indiana

Mission Statement

Our mission is students distinguished by achievement, knowledge, skills and character.

School Characteristics:

Grade Levels: 7–12
Locale: Suburb-large
Total Students: 1,228
Male-Female Ratio: 51:49
Student-Teacher Ratio: 22.7:1
Free Lunch Eligible: 5.5 %
Reduced-Price Lunch Eligible: 3.4%

Ethnicity	N	%
AmerInd/Alaskan	3	0.2
Asian	7	0.6
Black	1	0.1
Hispanic	12	1.0
White	1,187	98.1

General Information:

14600 Amstutz Road
Leo, IN 46765
(260) 446-0180
www.eacs.k12.in.us/lhs/
*US DOE Blue Ribbon School

Middle College High School
Santa Ana, California

Mission Statement

The mission of Middle College High School, a collaborative between the Santa Ana Unified School District and Santa Ana College, is to provide a supportive, academically challenging environment for underserved youth with high academic potential that leads not only to a rich high school education but also leads to independence and success in college and beyond.

School Characteristics:

Grade Levels: 9–12
Locale: City-large
Total Students: 310
Male-Female Ratio: 40:60
Student-Teacher Ratio: 24.6:1
Free Lunch Eligible: 48.3%
Reduced-Price Lunch Eligible: 18.3%

Ethnicity	N	%
AmerInd/Alaskan	0	0.0
Asian	9	2.9
Black	4	1.3
Hispanic	287	92.6
White	10	3.2

General Information:

1530 West 17th Street
Santa Ana, CA 92706
(714) 953-3900
www.sausd.us/Domain/2986
*US DOE Blue Ribbon School

Preuss UCSD
La Jolla, California

Mission Statement

The mission of the Preuss School is to improve educational practices and provide an intensive college preparatory school for low-income student populations, which are historically underrepresented on the campuses of the University of California. The mission will thereby further the outreach efforts of the University of California and its commitment to the San Diego community and to educational intervention. Additionally, the school will support the district's goal of reducing the achievement gap among under-represented students.

The Preuss School's goals also support the district's mission statement by emphasizing the following:

♦ Weekly staff development and team meetings for teachers focused on teaching and learning using analysis of lessons and student work.
♦ An innovative traditional liberal arts curriculum that emphasizes student understanding and literacy.
♦ Tutoring to ensure student achievement.
♦ A climate of high expectations and a strong academic culture.
♦ Use of University resources to enhance teaching and learning.
♦ A focus on personalization of instruction.

The Preuss School provides an environment where students are continually encouraged and empowered to develop a greater sense of confidence and self-worth through self-sufficiency and a sense of pride in their academic accomplishments. The school fosters a culture of high academic performance in an environment that encourages risk-taking, the art of questioning and logical and critical thinking. Graduates will be stimulated to enjoy lifelong intellectual curiosity and dedication to continued learning. The school encourages the involvement of community, family and other institutions to share responsibility for encouraging young people to develop both as scholars and citizens.

continued

School Characteristics:
Grade Levels: 6–12
Locale: City-large
Total Students: 755
Male-Female Ratio: 46:54
Student-Teacher Ratio: 19.4:1
Free Lunch Eligible: 99.6%
Reduced-Price Lunch Eligible: 0%

Ethnicity	N	%
AmerInd/Alaskan	1	0.1
Asian	160	21.2
Black	86	11.4
Hispanic	469	62.3
White	37	4.9

General Information:
9500 Gilman Drive
La Jolla, CA 92093
(858) 658-7404
http://preuss.ucsd.edu/
Newsweek's Best High Schools (2010)

Ridge High School
Basking Ridge, New Jersey

Mission Statement

The mission of Ridge High School is to prepare each student to be a knowledgeable and reputable member of society who functions with self-esteem, discipline, integrity, and compassion. In support of this mission, the faculty and administration are committed to:

♦ creating an orderly environment for students characterized by high expectations, respect for both academic and artistic excellence, personal achievement, and mutual respect.
♦ providing a strong academic program in all education areas.
♦ providing quality instruction in all classes.
♦ providing remedial assistance for students needing basic skill support.
♦ assisting each prospective graduate to enter college, advanced training, or the work force.
♦ maintaining close contact with parents and community.
♦ creating an environment for faculty characterized by collegiality, collaboration, inquiry, and respect for the knowledge base of the profession.

School Characteristics:
Grade Levels: 9–12
Locale: Suburb-large
Total Students: 1,697
Male-Female Ratio: 52:48
Student-Teacher Ratio: 12.1:1
Free Lunch Eligible: 0.5%
Reduced-Price Lunch Eligible: 0.2%

Ethnicity	N	%
AmerInd/Alaskan	3	0.2
Asian	235	13.8
Black	16	0.9
Hispanic	59	3.5
White	1,379	81.3
Two or more races	5	0.3

General Information:
268 South Finley Avenue
Basking Ridge, NJ 07920
(908) 204-2585
www1.bernardsboe.com/RidgeHighSchool/
*US DOE Blue Ribbon School

Rock Creek Jr./Sr. High School
St. George, Kansas

Mission Statement

Rock Creek Jr./Sr. High School will provide an orderly, supportive, quality learning environment to challenge all students to achieve, believe, dream, produce and relate to others with responsibility and integrity in a manner that credits themselves and society.

School Characteristics:

Grade Levels: 7–12
Locale: Rural-remote
Total Students: 377
Male-Female Ratio: 54:46
Student-Teacher Ratio: 12.3:1
Free Lunch Eligible: 14.6%
Reduced-Price Lunch Eligible: 11.9%

Ethnicity	N	%
AmerInd/Alaskan	1	0.3
Asian	3	0.8
Black	7	1.9
Hispanic	11	2.9
White	355	94.2

General Information:

9355 Flush Road
St. George, KS 66535
(785) 494-8591
www.rockcreekschools.org/vnews/display.v/SEC/Rock%20Creek%20JSHS
*US DOE Blue Ribbon School

School of Science and Engineering
Dallas, Texas

Mission Statement

The Science and Engineering Magnet High School is a learning community established to provide students with a rigorous college preparatory, academic and technical program relating to the sciences, mathematics and engineering fields.

School Characteristics:

Grade Levels: 9–12
Locale: City-large
Total Students: 399
Male-Female Ratio: 67:33
Student-Teacher Ratio: 14.9:1
Free Lunch Eligible: 42.6%
Reduced-Price Lunch Eligible: 12.3%

Ethnicity	N	%
AmerInd/Alaskan	2	0.5
Asian	30	7.5
Black	66	16.5
Hispanic	221	55.4
White	80	20.1

General Information:

1201 East Eighth Street
Dallas, TX 75203
(972) 925-5960
www.semagnetschool.org/
Newsweek's Best High Schools (2010)

School for the Talented and Gifted
Dallas, Texas

Mission Statement

Our mission is to take our students and provide them with the talents and skills to be accepted to the colleges/universities of their choice with the money to go there and to be successful at those institutions of higher learning.

School Characteristics:

Grade Levels: 9–12

Locale: City-large

Total Students: 211

Male-Female Ratio: 35:65

Student-Teacher Ratio: 12.5:1

Free Lunch Eligible: 19.4%

Reduced-Price Lunch Eligible: 8.1%

Ethnicity	N	%
AmerInd/Alaskan	0	0.0
Asian	15	7.1
Black	45	21.4
Hispanic	60	28.6
White	90	42.9

General Information:

1201 East Eighth Street

Dallas, TX 75203

(972) 925-5970

http://tagmagnet.org

Newsweek's Best High Schools (2010)

Thomas Jefferson High School for Science and Technology
Alexandria, Virginia

Mission Statement

The mission of Thomas Jefferson High School for Science and Technology is to provide students a challenging learning environment focused on math, science, and technology, to inspire joy at the prospect of discovery, and to foster a culture of innovation based on ethical behavior and the shared interests of humanity.

School Characteristics:

Grade Levels: 9–12
Locale: Suburb-large
Total Students: 1,815
Male-Female Ratio: 54:46
Student-Teacher Ratio: 16.0:1
Free Lunch Eligible: 0.7%
Reduced-Price Lunch Eligible: 0.6%

Ethnicity	N	%
AmerInd/Alaskan	6	0.4
Asian	753	44.2
Black	33	1.9
Hispanic	50	2.9
White	862	50.6

General Information:

6560 Braddock Road
Alexandria, VA 22312
(703) 750-8300
www.tjhsst.edu/
*US DOE Blue Ribbon School

Trion High School
Trion, Georgia

Mission Statement

To promote personal growth and leadership development through family and consumer sciences education. Focusing on the multiple roles of family member, wage earner, and community leader, members develop skills for life through—

- ◆ character development,
- ◆ creative and critical thinking;
- ◆ interpersonal communication;
- ◆ practical knowledge; and
- ◆ vocational preparation

School Characteristics:

Grade Levels: 9–12
Locale: Town-remote
Total Students: 360
Male-Female Ratio: 49:51
Student-Teacher Ratio: 13.0:1
Free Lunch Eligible: 11.4%
Reduced-Price Lunch Eligible: 6.1%

Ethnicity	N	%
AmerInd/Alaskan	0	0.0
Asian	5	1.4
Black	4	1.1
Hispanic	14	3.9
White	336	93.6

General Information:

919 Allgood St
Trion, GA 30753
(706) 734-7316
www.trionschools.org/index.php?option=com_content&view=category&layout=blog&id=140&Itemid=127&lang=en
*US DOE Blue Ribbon School

Vestavia Hills High School
Vestavia Hills, Alabama

Mission Statement

The mission of Vestavia Hills High School, a collaborative learning community with a continuing tradition of excellence, is to cultivate responsible and compassionate shapers of society by fostering personal growth through community service, charter development, and a rigorous, varied, relevant curriculum.

School Characteristics:

Grade Levels: 9–12
Locale: Suburb-large
Total Students: 1,678
Male-Female Ratio: 51:49
Student-Teacher Ratio: 13.9:1
Free Lunch Eligible: 2.9%
Reduced-Price Lunch Eligible: 1.6%

Ethnicity	N	%
AmerInd/Alaskan	4	0.2
Asian	81	4.8
Black	138	8.2
Hispanic	24	1.4
White	1,431	85.3

General Information:

2235 Lime Rock Road
Vestavia Hills, AL 35216
(205) 402-5250
www.vestavia.k12.al.us/VestaviaHigh/index.cfm
*US DOE Blue Ribbon School

West Lyon High School
Inwood, Iowa

Mission Statement

West Lyon School is committed to the service of the students entrusted to us. We strive for the fullest development and maturation of each child. We also recognize that the school is not the only institution that plays a vital role in the growth of young people. The home, church, law enforcement agencies, and social welfare institutions also have a major responsibility.

School Characteristics:

Grade Levels: 9–12
Locale: Rural-remote
Total Students: 217
Male-Female Ratio: 56:44
Student-Teacher Ratio: 10.6:1
Free Lunch Eligible: 11.5%
Reduced-Price Lunch Eligible: 12.9%

Ethnicity	N	%
AmerInd/Alaskan	1	0.5
Asian	1	0.5
Black	0	0.0
Hispanic	3	1.4
White	212	97.7

General Information:

1787 182nd Street
Inwood, IA 51240
(712) 753-4917
www.west-lyon.k12.ia.us/
*US DOE Blue Ribbon School

Bodine High School for International Affairs
Philadelphia, Pennsylvania

Mission Statement

The mission of the Home & School Association is to promote the interests of Bodine High School for International Affairs and its students. We strive to make a difference by aiding the school and helping to facilitate the development of a rich learning environment for our children.

School Characteristics:

Grade Levels: 9–12
Locale: City Large
Total Students: 561
Male-Female Ratio: 39:61
Student-Teacher Ratio: 21.1:1
Free Lunch Eligible: 39.0%
Reduced-Price Lunch Eligible: 4.6%

Ethnicity	N	%
AmerInd/Alaskan	0	0.0
Asian	71	12.8
Black	317	57.0
Hispanic	88	15.8
White	80	14.4

General Information:

1101 North 4th Street
Philadelphia, PA 19123
(215) 351-7332
www.bodine.phila.k12.pa.us/
*US DOE Blue Ribbon School

PART III

Analysis and Conclusions

15

Common and Unique Themes in School Mission Statements

In the previous chapters, we presented examples of school mission statements from a wide variety of American elementary, middle and high schools. A review of these chapters reveals that the schools in the United States show tremendous diversity with regard to their fundamental philosophies and primary missions. Indeed, the diversity can be so striking that the first question of interest to be addressed in this chapter is whether we see American schools converging in any broad way regarding the primary purposes of their schools. Given that every school represented here is similarly devoted to educating American children between five and eighteen years old, how different are the schools in their stated purposes and missions? In this chapter, we step back and take a broad view of the different themes and patterns we observed across all schools and within the different school types presented in each chapter.

Using the mission statement coding rubric we presented in Chapter 2, we analyzed the entire set of 111 mission statements presented in this book. As Figure 15.1 (page 154) illustrates, our analyses revealed that two-thirds of these school mission statements include at least some reference to emotional development, and the majority of schools also include reference to cognitive development. These results suggest that even across a broad range of school types, there is at least some consensus with regard to at least two broad purposes of schooling: emotional and cognitive development. These findings are consistent with our prior research using random samples of American schools (Stemler, Bebell, & Sonnabend, 2011).

FIGURE 15.1 Percentage of Schools in This Book (N = 111) Citing Each Major Theme

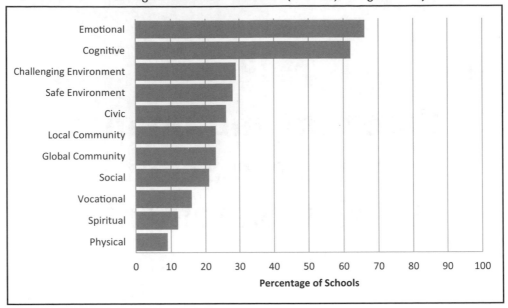

Although we observed that most schools in this book emphasize emotional (66 percent) and cognitive themes (62 percent) in their mission statements, a variety of other themes were also regularly found in school mission statements. Some themes, such as physical development, occurred more frequently in schools serving a particular type of student (e.g., elementary age students). Other themes, such as spiritual development, were observed frequently in some school types (e.g., parochial schools) but rarely found in other types of schools (e.g., public schools).

In the remainder of this chapter, we specifically examine the various themes articulated within each of the different types of school found in each chapter. This analysis will provide a basis of comparison across schools that serve different student bodies and espouse different educational philosophies.

Analysis by School Type

Public Elementary Schools

Across our sample of public elementary schools, the primary theme of mission statements involves providing a safe environment that fosters the emotional development of children (see Figure 15.2). Public elementary school

FIGURE 15.2 Percentage of Public Elementary Schools (N = 8) Citing Each Major Theme

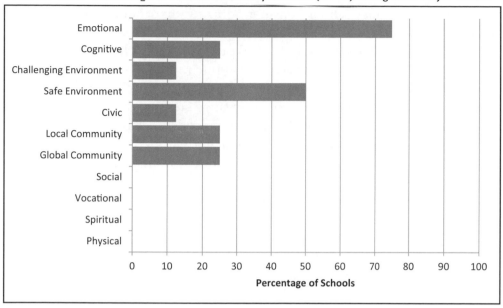

mission statements generally speak to the role of the school as a place to create a particular kind of environment (e.g., safe/nurturing) as well as the outcomes the school hopes to cultivate (e.g., fostering students' emotional development). For example, the mission statement of Providence Elementary School in Utah provides a fairly prototypical example of a public elementary school's dual emphasis:

> The mission of Providence Elementary School is to establish a cooperative school-wide community where children are eager to learn, are successful and happy; a school where children meet new challenges with confidence in their own self-worth and the worth of others.
>
> —Providence Elementary School
> Providence, Utah (p. 28)

Public Middle Schools

As in public elementary schools, emotional development is still a dominant theme in many public middle schools (55 percent of our sample); however, cognitive development is mentioned nearly as often, so that these twin goals tend to stand side by side (see Figure 15.3, page 156). In addition, the creation of a safe school environment continues to be a dominant theme; however, the creation of a challenging school environment was also observed more often than in the elementary schools. Furthermore, middle schools often include an increased emphasis on students' integration into the local community via collaborative partnerships (36 percent of all public middle school). Some middle schools (18 percent of our sample) also explicitly recognize the importance of social development as a key outcome for this particular population of students. Examined collectively, these findings support the notion of middle schools as a transitional bridge between the needs of elementary school students and the demands placed on high school students. The McLaughlin Middle School in Manchester, New Hampshire, provides an example that is somewhat unusual with regard to the number of themes integrated into the mission statement, but that clearly indicates the vast range of purposes the school aims to serve.

> McLaughlin Middle School is a school that understands the intellectual, physical, social, and emotional needs of pre and early adolescents, cares for them and prepares them for academic success. These future citizens are the life blood, hope and future of this city, the nation, and the world. We recognize that it is our responsibility to provide the future generations with an education that will meet their needs in a constantly changing world. We also affirm that the process of education is a partnership between students, education, parents,

FIGURE 15.3 Percentage of Public Middle Schools (N = 11) Citing Each Major Theme

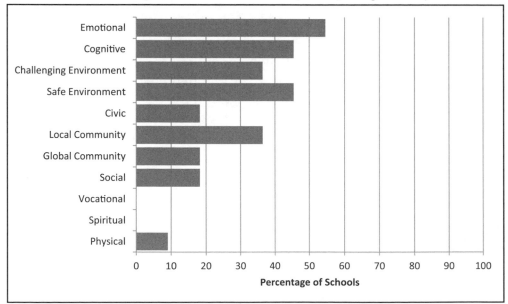

and the community and is based on mutual respect and cooperation. Education is the development of the whole person which includes intellectual, social, physical and emotional components. The school recognizes the individual abilities, differences, and interest of students and attempts to provide ways for them to understand themselves; to develop self-discipline, self-confidence, and a good self image; to develop their entire person to the epitome of their abilities, ever striving to achieve high standards and worthy goals.

—Henry J. McLaughlin Middle School
Manchester, New Hampshire (p. 33)

Public High Schools

Across the public high schools we include here, the most dominant theme cited across mission statements relates to civic development and students' successful integration into their local communities (see Figure 15.4). Cognitive development and emotional development are also frequently observed themes in public high school mission statements. The strong emphasis on students' civic development appears to be a rather distinctive feature of public high schools in America. No other school type similarly emphasizes civic development as frequently as the public high schools. The mission statement

FIGURE 15.4 Percentage of Public High Schools (N=11) Citing Each Major Theme

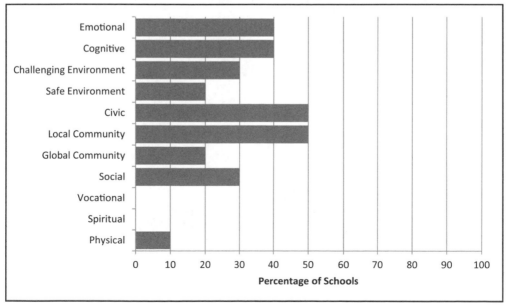

of Bentonville High School in Arkansas provides a succinct and fairly representative example of the way in which citizenship is highlighted within high school mission statements.

> The mission of Bentonville High School is to provide our students with opportunities to obtain the skills needed to become productive, responsible citizens, capable of making positive contributions to a changing society.
>
> —Bentonville High School
> Bentonville, Arkansas (p. 43)

We also observed that there is a decreased emphasis in public high school mission statements on providing a safe/nurturing environment (22 percent)—a theme cited in approximately half of the elementary (50 percent) and middle school mission statements (45 percent).

Vocational/Career/Technical Education Schools

Across the vocational/career/technical education schools, we were not especially surprised to observe a strong emphasis on career-oriented themes (see Figure 15.5). However, two-thirds of vocational/CTE schools from our

FIGURE 15.5 Percentage of Vocational/Career/Technical Ed Schools (N = 9) Citing Each Major Theme

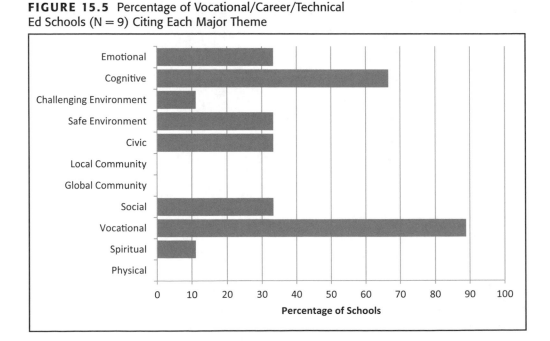

sample additionally emphasized cognitive development themes in their mission statements. Given that vocational schools typically serve high school age students, it appears that most vocational schools jointly emphasize academic achievement (cognitive development) and job preparation. The mission statement of North County Trade Tech School in Vista, California, illustrates this balance:

> To graduate students with a strong blend of academic and workforce competencies necessary for future success in post-secondary education and in the building and construction industry.
>
> —North County Trade Tech School
> Vista, California (p. 57)

Although many vocational schools in the US are public high schools, we observed some that are privately operated. The Mercy Vocational High School in Philadelphia, Pennsylvania, provides an interesting example from privately affiliated vocational high schools. In this example, we note that the school incorporates cognitive and vocational elements into its mission statement, as well as several other key themes:

> Mercy Vocational High School is a private, urban vocational high school sponsored by the Sisters of Mercy. The school's mission is to provide a Catholic education to those students whose educational and career goals are best served by a quality, comprehensive academic/ vocational secondary school program. Students acquire marketable skills to enter immediately into their career vocation or to pursue post-secondary education. As a school Community we seek to live the Gospel in word and action. We place the highest priority on the spiritual and moral development of our students and their service to others.
>
> —Mercy Vocational High School
> Philadelphia, Pennsylvania (p. 55)

Magnet Schools

The themes across the magnet school mission statements we collected were fairly consistent with the overall sample of schools. We observed a dominant emphasis on emotional development followed by cognitive development (see Figure 15.6, page 160). From a qualitative perspective, however, there is strong emphasis on creativity and artistic achievement in the mission statements of the magnet schools. These emphases likely reflect the magnet school tradition of enhanced curricular offerings related to arts and technology.

FIGURE 15.6 Percentage of Magnet Schools (N = 9) Citing Each Major Theme

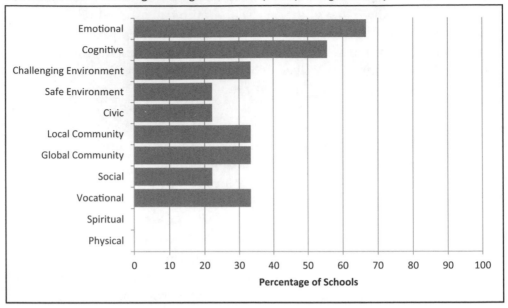

About half the magnet schools also emphasize the importance of connecting instruction to state curriculum standards. An emphasis on vocational/career preparation is also prevalent in about one-third of the mission statements examined. The Richard J. Kinsella Magnet School of Performing Arts in Hartford, Connecticut, provides an illustrative example:

> At the Richard J. Kinsella Magnet School of Performing Arts, we view each child as a competent and resourceful problem solver. Our mission is to provide each child with an enriched educational environment, which fosters artistic, independent and critical thinking through Arts integrated instruction. We are committed to celebrating student, staff, and community diversity while promoting life-long learning, love of the Arts and developing persons of commendable moral character.
> —Richard J. Kinsella Magnet School of Performing Arts
> Hartford, Connecticut (p. 72)

Charter Schools

As one of the fastest growing school types in the US today, charter schools have mission statements that nearly always focus on some dimension of students' cognitive development (see Figure 15.7, page 162). When comparing charter schools to traditional public schools, it is striking that only 13 percent of charter schools in our sample include any reference to civic development. Our sample reflects the fact that some charter schools follow a curriculum similar to typical public schools, while others are highly specialized. For example, the Rilke Schule German School of Arts & Sciences, a charter school in Anchorage, Alaska, provides a fascinating example of a public charter school with a highly specialized curricular approach:

> Rilke Schule German School of Arts & Sciences is a K through 8 public charter school that provides an outstanding education focused on high academic achievement by engaging each child through an enriched immersion language curriculum taught primarily in German.
> —Rilke Schule German School of Arts & Sciences
> Anchorage, Alaska (p. 83)

Other charter schools, such as the Academy of Business and Leadership Education in Saint Augustine, Florida, suggest many of the same themes found in typical public school mission statements but with their own highly specialized approach and emphasis:

> ABLE will strive to inspire and cultivate the innate leadership and creative impulses within all children, developing educated, caring and responsible world citizens. This vision will be pursued at multiple learning sites to provide small, flexible learning communities in safe, challenging and caring educational environments. Innovative teaching strategies will emphasize enjoyable and relevant educational experiences in which the fundamentals of entrepreneurship and leadership will be integrated into all levels and subject areas. Students will master basic skills at a high level of competence while acquiring knowledge and skills in problem solving and decision-making. Our programs will be characterized by the cooperative presence and unified support of families, businesses, and educational and civic groups with whom our students will interact. Emphasis on self-sufficiency, civic responsibility and a passion for lifelong learning will develop responsible leaders for the 21st Century.
> —Academy for Business and Leadership Education
> Saint Augustine, Florida (p. 76)

Qualitatively, we found that charter school mission statements tend to include references to "creativity" much more frequently than in the mission statements of other school types. Lastly, many charter school mission statements

FIGURE 15.7 Percentage of Charter Schools (N = 8) Citing Each Major Theme

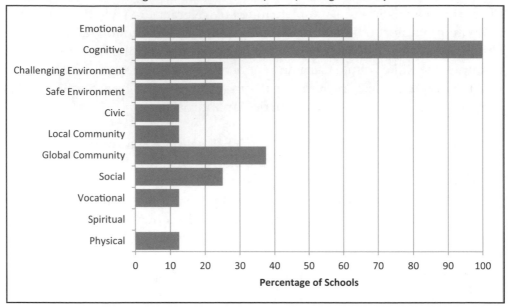

made frequent reference to the world as a "competitive" place, reflecting the underlying free-market value system associated with many charter schools.

Native American/Tribal Schools

Native American/Tribal schools provide an example of a publicly funded American school system that serves a specific community and student population. Similar to most other school types, we observed an emphasis on cognitive and emotional development in the Native American/Tribal schools (see Figure 15.8). However, across the small sample of Native American/Tribal schools examined here, the theme of social development was observed more regularly than in other school types. The Native American/Tribal schools also tend to clearly emphasize the important role that the individual student plays in his or her own education, as illustrated by the mission statement of Kayenta Middle School in Arizona:

> It is the individual's responsibility to attain a successful life. Thinking, planning, learning, working together. This is what we want for you; through guidance we will get there together.
>
> —Kayenta Middle School
> Kayenta, Arizona (p. 88)

FIGURE 15.8 Percentage of Native American/Tribal Schools (N = 5) Citing Each Major Theme

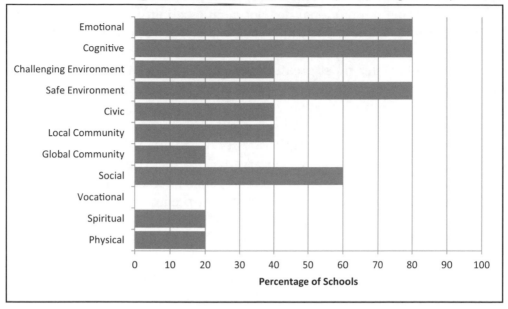

Similarly, Native American/Tribal school mission statements often emphasize the importance of more holistic educational approach to education by including references to cognitive, emotional, social, and civic components. The mission statement of Chief Leschi Schools in Puyallup, Washington, provides one example:

> Chief Leschi Schools' mission in cooperation with the Puyallup Tribe, the Native American community and the community as a greater whole is to create challenging opportunities to educate students in an atmosphere of mutual trust and respect. It is our common mission to inspire each student to achieve personal growth and cultural pride, to value life long learning, and to become a responsible contributing citizen of their community, the Puyallup Nation, Washington State, and the United States of America in a complex and ever changing world.
> —Chief Leschi School
> Puyallup, Washington (p. 86)

Parochial Schools

As private alternatives to public schools, parochial schools can be found across the nearly entire American educational landscape. Across the parochial

schools we examined here, 100% of their mission statements include a reference to the theme of emotional development (see Figure 15.9). In addition,
nearly all schools make explicit reference to the schools' role in fostering the
cognitive development of their students. However, parochial school mission statements differ most greatly from public schools in their inclusion
of a spiritual development theme (observed in 78 percent of parochial mission statements). From a qualitative perspective, two common elements are
emphasized across the parochial schools: helping students discover their
own unique God-given talents/gifts and service to others.

Even in our small sample, we observed a surprising amount of diversity
within the parochial schools. Some schools, such as the Archmere Academy
in Claymont, Delaware, take a more inclusive approach and use their mission
statements to emphasize a respect for diversity and to welcome students of
different faiths:

> Archmere Academy is a Roman Catholic, independent, college pre-
> paratory school inspired by the Norbertine tradition and a heritage of
> committed faculty, alumni, families, and friends. Archmere welcomes
> faculty and students of diverse religious and cultural backgrounds.
> Through dedication to academic excellence, social development, com-
> munity service, and faith reflection, Archmere focuses on the edu-
> cation of the whole student. This philosophy encourages and sup-
> ports the unique qualities and differences of students in achieving the

FIGURE 15.9 Percentage of Parochial Schools (N = 9) Citing Each Major Theme

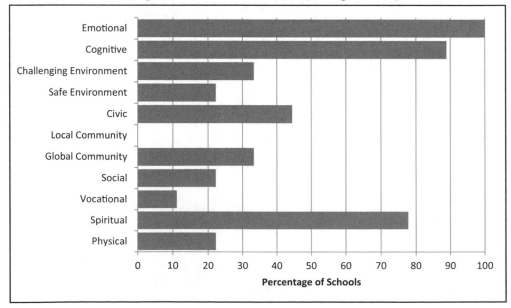

maximum level of their abilities. Understanding their moral obligation to the global community, young men and women graduate from Archmere prepared for college, career and vocation in life.

—Archmere Academy
Claymont, Delaware (p. 93)

Other parochial schools, such as Alabama's Montgomery Catholic Preparatory School, focus more singularly on their own approach, devotion, and perspective:

Montgomery Catholic Preparatory School is an integral part of the Catholic Church's mission to proclaim the gospel of Jesus Christ. As an adult community, we share in the responsibility to prepare students for college and beyond while helping them grow to become persons of faith, virtue and wisdom.

—Montgomery Catholic Preparatory School
Montgomery, Alabama (p. 98)

Waldorf Schools

As was generally the case across school types, nearly all the Waldorf school mission statements in our sample include both cognitive and emotional development themes (see Figure 15.10, page 166). However, the way these cognitive and emotional themes are articulated by the Waldorf schools differs from other school types we examined. In particular, cognitive themes emphasized by the Waldorf schools tend to include references to "developmentally appropriate" learning opportunities, student initiative, and fostering independent thinking and did not tend to include reference to core curriculum standards. The emotional development themes focused on respect, gratitude, and strength of will. Another interesting result we observed while examining the Waldorf school mission statements was the emphasis on "cooperation," which contrasted with the emphasis on competition and the "competitive world" espoused by many charter schools. The Waldorf schools were also somewhat unique in their emphasis on helping students develop a purpose-driven life. Finally, there was also a focus on physical development in Waldorf schools that was rarely mentioned across other school types. The mission statement of Desert Marigold School in Phoenix, Arizona provides a prototypical example:

Inspired by Rudolf Steiner's Waldorf Education system, the mission of Desert Marigold School is to provide an educational context that

FIGURE 15.10 Percentage of Waldorf Schools (N = 7) Citing Each Major Theme

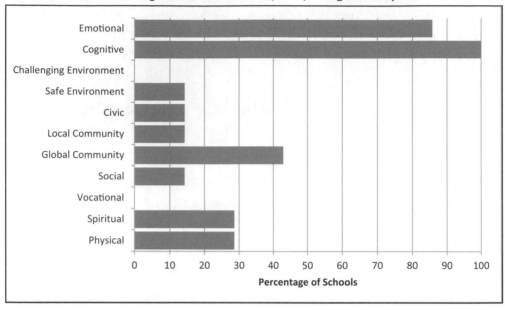

emphasizes not only intellectual achievement, but also the imaginative, artistic, and moral growth of its students. By addressing their heads, hands and hearts, the school will encourage students to be life-long learners and independent thinkers as well as self motivated, self-disciplined, creative, adaptable and responsible individuals.

We seek to establish and maintain a school that provides an individualized, nurturing approach to educating its students, preparing them not only for higher education, but for the rest of their lives. We will require and use an active partnership of teachers, families and the community, as well as a continued affiliation with the world-wide Waldorf movement to achieve the following goals:

1. To ensure each child's excellence in core academic skills by providing a curriculum enlivened with the arts of painting, music, drama, movement, singing, sculpture and hand work.
2. To educate according to age and development, so that learning and growth are united.
3. To present the curriculum in multiple and integrated ways, so students have many different opportunities to learn concepts, as well as see the relationship to the larger whole.
4. To nourish the spirit of curiosity so that students continue to learn long after the end of formal training.

5. To encourage fundamental values and life skills, including responsibility, perseverance, integrity, self-discipline, trust-worthiness, craftsmanship, friendship and compassion.

6. To make available this quality of education for all ethnic and socioeconomic sectors in our community.

—Desert Marigold School
Phoenix, Arizona (p. 104)

Montessori Schools

Across the Montessori schools we examined, the most frequently cited themes in the mission statements relate to emotional development, followed by cognitive development and the provision of a safe environment (see Figure 15.11, page 168). Compared to those of other school types, Montessori mission statements are notable for their complete absence of civic development themes. Instead, the Montessori school mission statements nearly always focus on themes related to the development and fostering of each student's individuality. Similarly, Montessori mission statements often highlight the belief and emphasis on meeting a range of learning styles and temperaments. The Chesterfield Montessori School of Chesterfield, Missouri, mission statement provides one example:

> Chesterfield Montessori School offers an authentic Montessori education that honors children's individuality. Our peaceful environment and compassionate staff nurtures respect for self and others, fosters a strong sense of community, and stimulates independent thinking. Students carry with them a solid record of academic achievement, a belief in the dignity of work, and a sense of responsibility for their own development as happy and productive human beings.
>
> —Chesterfield Montessori School
> Chesterfield, Missouri (p. 114)

A second interesting example comes from the Montessori School at Holy Rosary in Cleveland, Ohio. In this second mission statement, we observe a combination of the Montessori philosophy embedded within the context of a parochial school philosophy. Also, the Holy Rosary mission statement highlights an element that was explicit across many Montessori schools: the belief that the *school's* role is to adapt instruction to student needs and abilities.

The Montessori School at Holy Rosary is dedicated to providing outstanding educational instruction by discovering and awakening

FIGURE 15.11 Percentage of Montessori Schools (N = 7) Citing Each Major Theme

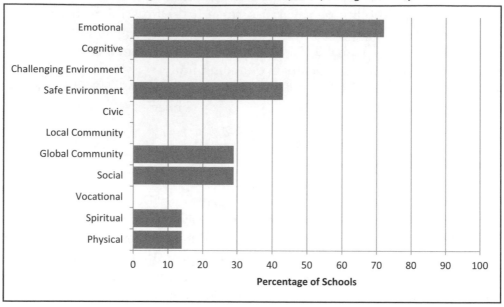

children's emerging potential and carefully cultivating the development of their innate talents and abilities. We are vitally committed to providing excellence in education to the children of Greater Cleveland through the philosophy and techniques of the Montessori method, provided in a Catholic atmosphere, enriched by the values of love, respect, and justice. The Montessori School at Holy Rosary is established to serve all children, regardless of race or creed, and is uniquely devoted to enhancing the vitality of Holy Rosary Parish and the Little Italy community.

—Montessori School at Holy Rosary
Cleveland, Ohio (p. 116)

Apple Schools of Distinction

Within the Apple Schools of Distinction, we observed mission statements that are fairly similar to those in public schools. Consistent with most schools, the joint emphasis of the majority of school mission statements was cognitive and emotional development (see Figure 15.12). In other words, despite receiving accolades for using technology to advance teaching and learning, the majority of these school mission statements were no different than typical public schools. Two elements found in this sample were not typically found in other

FIGURE 15.12 Percentage of Apple Schools of Distinction (N = 9) Citing Each Major Theme

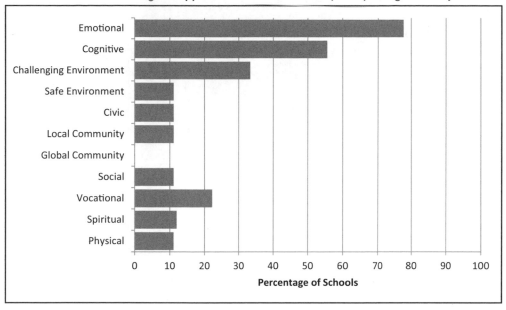

school types, however. The first element includes an emphasis in the mission statement on how the school adopted and/or integrated technology. The second element emphasizes new skills for the future. The Washington Middle School in Kenosha, Wisconsin, has a mission statement that explicitly reflects both these themes:

> To empower all students to become motivated independent thinkers prepared to excel at the next level, by creating an environment that provides a quality education which integrates technology, expects family involvement, and implements research-based instruction. We believe that laptop learning engages our students in more dynamic ways, allowing them to explore world-wide information sources, enhance academic and fine arts skills, and organize their work more effectively. We are developing 21st Century learners.
>
> —Washington Middle School
> Kenosha, Wisconsin (p. 127)

Award Winning Schools

Across the mission statements for schools receiving either a US Department of Education Blue Ribbon Award or a rating by *Newsweek Magazine* as a "Best

FIGURE 15.13 Percentage of Award Winning Schools (N = 19) Citing Each Major Theme

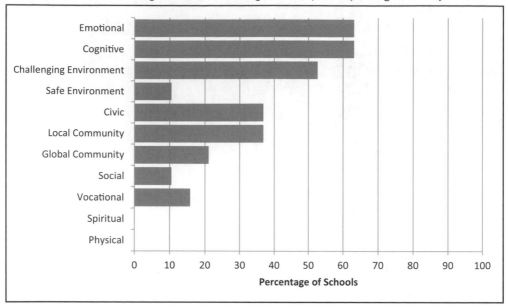

High School," we observed fairly similar themes to those in typical public schools. In particular, we found a strong emphasis on emotional development, cognitive development and the provision of a challenging environment, citizenship and integration into local community (see Figure 15.13). The mission statement of Thomas Jefferson High School for Science and Technology in Alexandria, Virginia, succinctly expresses these themes:

> The mission of Thomas Jefferson High School for Science and Technology is to provide students a challenging learning environment focused on math, science, and technology, to inspire joy at the prospect of discovery, and to foster a culture of innovation based on ethical behavior and the shared interests of humanity.
> —Thomas Jefferson High School for Science and Technology
> Alexandria, Virginia (p. 145)

Conclusion

In evaluating the content found across the 111 school mission statements presented in this book, we found that most American schools share in common some broad beliefs about the primary purpose(s) of schooling, at least as expressed by their mission statements. Despite their differences, most of the mission statements we examined highlighted at least two themes: cognitive development and emotional development of their students. These two themes emerge with a high degree of frequency across nearly all school types. To be clear, our goal as authors is to be descriptive and not pass judgment as to the superiority or inferiority of any one school type. However, we were also interested in observing the variety of other purposes that different schools across America also purport to serve.

Across public high school mission statements, the most frequently observed theme is civic development, whereas not a single Montessori school in our sample mentions the civic development of students. Most parochial schools include a focus on spiritual development, as one might expect, but we observed two different types of parochial school mission statements: one in which enrollment by students of diverse ethnic and religious backgrounds is encouraged and another type that is more exclusive.

Montessori schools hold emotional development and the provision of a safe and nurturing environment as their primary aim, whereas the US DOE Blue Ribbon schools tend to emphasize the provision of a challenging environment and the cognitive and emotional development of their students as key objectives.

One of the most fascinating contrasts we observed comes from a comparison of the mission statements of KIPP schools (a subset of charter schools) and Waldorf schools. Both school types primarily tend to serve students in kindergarten through eighth grade, and both school types universally have mission statements that express cognitive themes. However, KIPP schools and Waldorf schools' perspectives toward cognitive development is often quite different. KIPP school mission statements generally emphasize "knowledge, skills, and character traits needed for success in college and life" and further stress the idea that students are expected to attend college. The linguistic focus in these statements tends to be on the product of education (e.g., degrees, jobs) rather than the process. In addition, there is often an emphasis on the concept of preparing students for a "competitive world" and frequent mention of the importance of developing students who could be "agents of change." The KIPP Academy of Opportunity in Los Angeles, California, provides a prototypical KIPP mission statement:

> KAO's mission is to ensure that students develop the academic skills, character, and intellectual habits necessary to succeed in competitive high schools, colleges, and the world beyond. Our six guiding principles are: respect, hard work, results, constant learning, determination, and teamwork.
>
> —KIPP Academy of Opportunity
> Los Angeles, California (p. 81)

By contrast, our review of Waldorf school mission statements reveals a different focus. We found few, if any, mentions of college preparation in Waldorf school mission statements. In addition, Waldorf school mission statements tend to focus much more on the process of education rather than the product. Specifically, they tend to emphasize the importance of developmentally appropriate tasks, independent thinking, personal initiative, social relations (community and friendship), emotional development (respect, gratitude, strength of will), and art. Across Waldorf school mission statements, there is an emphasis on "the whole child," including physical development—a component that is rarely noted in other school types. Finally, the Waldorf school mission statements consistently emphasize cooperation as opposed to competition. The Bay School in Blue Hill, Maine, provides an example of a Waldorf school with many of these themes:

> The Bay School's mission is to provide an education that engages and nurtures the whole child, inspiring a balanced growth of heart, mind, body and spirit. We are committed to developing in our students' inner confidence, responsibility, self-motivation, a love of learning, imagination, creativity and intellectual clarity. The educational ideals and values of the school, rooted in the Waldorf tradition, create a community of children, alumni, parents and faculty imbued with reverence for others and the natural world.
>
> —The Bay School
> Blue Hill, Maine (p. 108)

Again, the point of contrasting these two mission statements is not to make any judgment as to which philosophy is superior. Indeed, the purpose of the book is to objectively reflect on the many different approaches and aims that school hold. In fact, the examples of KIPP and Waldorf schools demonstrate how school systems driven by two very different educational philosophies peacefully coexist within the American educational landscape. Furthermore, each enjoys popular support from different constituents. One of our major goals with this book is to illustrate that there are many school types in the United States that each have their own systematic and subtle differences in emphasis. For educators and school leaders, these examples also provide direct examples of how schools communicate their purpose to the world via their school mission statements.

Our personal belief is that no single educational philosophy or approach can be "best" suited for a nation with such wide-ranging aspirations and a diverse population. Indeed, schools with the most effective mission statements are going to be those that best serve their constituents, namely the students, parents, teachers, administration, and greater community. A mission statement from a rural vocational high school *should* have distinct themes from a parochial urban elementary school. An effective mission statement must first meet the needs of its own community. In the final chapter, we discuss how to go about crafting a school mission statement that accurately and effectively indicates what your own school values.

16

Crafting Your Own School Mission Statement

This chapter is intended to be a practical guide for educators and school leaders looking for specific language to use within the context of their own mission statements. Over the course of our research, we have been struck by just how few resources are available for educators and school leaders engaged in the process of reflecting upon their educational mission. How can we be so articulate about curricular decisions, yet struggle with the more fundamental questions of school purpose? We believe the school mission statement can be a useful vehicle by which a school can communicate its philosophy and fundamental values to a broad audience. Not all schools take full advantage of this opportunity.

In developing a school mission statement, the first step is to consider what themes are the most central to your own school's purpose. Our list of the 11 most common themes we have observed provides an easy starting point. The next step is to determine which aspects of each theme you wish to emphasize. The example mission statements presented in this book include schools that use very broad language as well as those with more specific language. Even within a given theme, schools can articulate their themes and ideas into the format of a mission statement in many different ways.

In this chapter, we highlight specific language from actual mission statements for a variety of different themes. For each central theme, we present selected examples of mission statements that illustrate some of the most common and interesting ways pertinent mission statements from a given theme can express these different elements of their vision and purpose. In addition, we highlight key words and phrases often associated with each of 11 themes and the different aspects of those themes. Finally, in an effort to allow the reader quick access to the full context of school mission statements that are relevant to a particular theme, we provide an index listing each of the schools in this book that incorporates each theme. In this chapter, we present each of the 11 themes in the order of the frequency with which they occur across the 111 school mission statements found in this book.

Emotional Development

The most frequently invoked theme found across all the school mission statements in this book is student's emotional development. Emotional development is a very broad theme, and therefore it is perhaps not surprising that schools use a variety of ways to emphasize its importance in their mission statements. Summarizing our research on school mission statements, we have identified five aspects of emotional development that American schools commonly express in their school mission statements:

1. Specific Character Traits
2. Love of Learning
3. Moral and Ethical Development
4. Existential Values
5. Environment Elements

Specific Character Traits

In many school mission statements, emotional development relates to the idea of inculcating positive character traits such as self-discipline, independence, resourcefulness, and integrity. For example, the Cardinal Newman School in Columbia, South Carolina, provides several clear examples of the character traits it attempts to cultivate within its student body:

> With origins dating to 1858, Cardinal Newman School, a diocesan, coeducational, college preparatory secondary school serving grades 7 through 12, exists for the purpose of providing Catholic education of the highest quality to children of residents of the greater Columbia community. With an emphasis on the Catholic tradition of education—strong academics, a dedication to service, and traditional Catholic, Christian values, Cardinal Newman School provides a safe and structured environment which challenges all students to achieve personal excellence in every way. Inspired by the community belief in divine providence and love, Cardinal Newman students will become self-disciplined learners who also demonstrate respect, integrity,

responsibility, and a sense of justice as they prepare to live lives of truth, integrity, and fidelity—VERITAS, INTEGRITAS, FIDELITAS.

—Cardinal Newman School
Columbia, South Carolina (Parochial School, p. 95)

Following are examples of the language that different school mission statements use in relation to the development of character traits:

◆ Develop self-discipline, self-confidence, and good self-image
◆ Develop self-directed learners
◆ Develop motivated, inquisitive students
◆ Develop happy and productive human beings
◆ Develop resourceful students
◆ Develop students who are sensitive and aware
◆ Develop students who are respectful of themselves and others
◆ Develop students who are competent, confident, productive, and responsible young adults
◆ Foster independence and individuality
◆ Promote inner strength and determination
◆ Promote self-esteem
◆ Promote compassion and moral strength
◆ Our students carry with them a strong belief in the dignity of work

Love of Learning

The second way we have observed schools portray emotional development in their mission statements relates to fostering a love of learning and an enthusiasm for knowledge in their students. In fact, developing student's "love of learning" is one of the most frequently occurring sentiments describing emotional development across American school mission statements. Indeed, mission statements from schools serving all grade levels often include text on the role that the school plays—or should play—in creating enthusiasm for learning. The mission statement of the Casa Dei Bambini school in Marietta, Georgia, captures the essence of this theme:

Casa's mission is to motivate its students from within by a natural curiosity and love for knowledge. The goal of education should not be to fill the child with facts but rather to cultivate his/her own natural desire to learn.

—Casa Dei Bambini
Marietta, Georgia (Montessori School, p. 113)

Common expressions and excerpts from school mission statements describing love of learning follow:

- ◆ Develop well-rounded, enthusiastic, and self-motivated learners
- ◆ Develop and maintain a spirit of joy in learning, cooperation in doing, and optimism for success and the future
- ◆ Instill a desire for lifelong learning
- ◆ Instill a love of learning
- ◆ Encourage enthusiasm for learning
- ◆ Foster a positive attitude toward school
- ◆ Motivate students from within by a natural curiosity and love for knowledge

Moral and Ethical Development

A third way that emotional development is expressed in many school mission statements relates to the emphasis on a school's role in cultivating students' character, or their moral and ethical development. This theme does not focus on spiritual development or a particular set of religious values, such as the Christian values emphasized by many parochial schools. Rather, moral and ethical development highlights more general emotional development, including self-reliance, moral character, and ethical responsibility. The mission statement of the Academe of the Oaks in Decatur, Georgia, provides an illustrative example:

> Adolescents today are inheriting a world with staggering challenges. To meet those challenges and solve ever more complex problems, our young men and women will need a strong sense of moral and ethical responsibility, tremendous creativity, inner strength, and the ability to work with each other in a global context.
>
> At Academe of the Oaks, our mission is to re-define the high school experience by educating our students to be resourceful, clear, and flexible thinkers, capable of making profound and positive contributions to the fast-changing world they inherit.
>
> —Academe of the Oaks
> Decatur, Georgia (Waldorf School, p. 103)

Generally, mission statements concerning moral and ethical development make an explicit attempt to instruct students about a general set of ethical values that transcend religious categories. Following are specific examples of how schools typically describe their moral and ethical foundations in their mission statements:

- ◆ Develop moral character in students
- ◆ Develop persons of commendable moral character
- ◆ Develop the intellect and character of students
- ◆ Instill moral and ethical responsibility
- ◆ Provide value-centered education
- ◆ Students will be self-reliant
- ◆ Students will become people of sound character
- ◆ Our school will promote ethical behavior

Existential Values

A fourth way we have seen schools express the importance of emotional development in mission statements relates to their focus on existential values, such as meaning and purpose in life, reaching one's own potential, and recognizing a set of basic human rights. The mission statement of the Honolulu, Hawaii, Waldorf School provides an example that captures many of these sentiments:

> Honolulu Waldorf School provides an education that fosters in each child a sense of meaning and purpose in life, and the confidence to meet his or her individual destiny.
>
> We recognize and welcome the unique gifts brought by each child we serve. We are committed to supporting each child in his or her intellectual, physical, emotional, and spiritual development by offering a will-based curriculum that integrates academic, practical, experiential, and artistic work. We educate each child so that he or she will contribute to the future of the world with clear and creative thinking, compassion and moral strength, and the courage to initiate change.
>
> We are inspired and guided in our work by the educational and spiritual insights of Rudolf Steiner and the continually growing body of research in anthroposphy, which maintains that the highest goal of education is the realization of responsible human freedom.
>
> —Honolulu Waldorf School
> Honolulu, Hawaii (Waldorf School, p. 107)

Additional examples of language used in school mission statements that focus on existential values follow:

- ◆ Challenge students to maximize their growth emotionally

- Challenge students to become who they want to be
- Challenge students to reach their full potential
- Develop students who understand the emotional needs of others
- Offer students an education that will enhance their personal lives
- Inspire each student to achieve personal growth and cultural pride
- Inspire students to demonstrate respect for self, others, and environment
- Foster in each child a sense of meaning and purpose in life
- Foster balanced growth of heart, mind, body, and spirit
- Provide students with the confidence to meet their destiny
- Help everyone develop a sense of the goodness, self-worth, and dignity of every person

Environment Elements

The final way that schools invoke emotional development in their mission statements emphasizes the school environment rather than the individual student. The focus within these mission statements is on creating a particular type of environment that will help foster the emotional development of students. Dynamite Montessori school in Cave Creek, Arizona, provides an example:

> Dynamite Montessori is a joyful place where children's spontaneity is expressed, where community is fostered, and respect is practiced. It is a safe place where the wonders of nature are discovered, and people experience kindness as the powerful force it is. Ours is a place where bilingual education is pursued, strong bodies are nurtured, lifelong friendships are formed, and the love of learning never wanes.
>
> —Dynamite Montessori
> Cave Creek, Arizona (Montessori School, p. 115)

Other examples from school mission statements describing the school environment follow:

- Provide an education that is based on the process of mutual respect and cooperation
- Foster the developmentally appropriate awakening of thinking, feeling, and willing
- Facilitate the fullest development and maturation of each child

Schools including the Emotional Development
theme in their mission statements:

Page #	School Name	School Type
103	Academe of the Oaks, GA	Waldorf
66	Academic Magnet HS, SC	Magnet
76	Academy for Business and Leadership, FL	Charter
67	Advanced Technologies Academy, NV	Magnet
93	Archmere Academy, DE	Parochial
112	Austin Montessori School, TX	Montessori
130	BASIS, AZ	Award Winning School
108	The Bay School, ME	Waldorf
46	Bossier High School, LA	Public High School
94	Brophy College Prep, AZ	Parochial
95	Cardinal Newman School, SC	Parochial
113	Casa Dei Bambini, GA	Montessori
114	Chesterfield Montessori School, MO	Montessori
86	Chief Leschi School, WA	Native American
132	Columbiana HS, OH	Award Winning School
77	Community Roots Charter School, NY	Charter
78	Compass Charter School, ID	Charter
120	Del Mar Middle School, CA	Apple Distinguished School
104	Desert Marigold School, AZ	Waldorf
22	DeSoto Central Elementary School, MS	Public Elementary School
23	Doña Ana Elementary School, NM	Public Elementary School
115	Dynamite Montessori, AZ	Montessori
134	Eastside HS, FL	Award Winning School
121	Echo Lake ES, WA	Apple Distinguished School
106	Emerson Waldorf School, NC	Waldorf
122	Empire HS, AZ	Apple Distinguished School
96	Father Gabriel Richard Catholic HS, MI	Parochial
69	Forest Lake Elementary School, SC	Magnet
87	Gila Crossing Community School, AZ	Native American
32	Glen Crest Middle School, IL	Public Middle School
33	Henry J. McLaughlin Jr. Middle School, NH	Public Middle School
107	Honolulu Waldorf School, HI	Waldorf
123	Howard Elementary School, OR	Apple Distinguished School

Page #	School Name	School Type
25	Jerome Stamply Elementary School, MS	Public Elementary School
97	Jesuit HS, OR	Parochial
81	KIPP Academy of Opportunity, CA	Charter
82	KIPP Sunshine Peak Academy, CO	Charter
136	Lakeville North HS, MN	Award Winning School
137	Leo Junior/Senior HS, IN	Award Winning School
124	Lilla G. Frederick Pilot Middle School, MA	Apple Distinguished School
55	Mercy Vocational HS, PA	Vocational
116	Montessori School at Holy Rosary, OH	Montessori
98	Montgomery Catholic Prep, AL	Parochial
48	Montpelier High School, VT	Public High School
89	Nay Ah Shing School, MN	Native American
71	Normal Park Museum Magnet, TN	Magnet
90	Nuweetooun School, RI	Native American
58	Oakland Technical HS, CA	Vocational
27	Parkside Elementary, WY	Public Elementary School
139	Preuss UCSD, CA	Award Winning School
28	Providence Elementary School, UT	Public Elementary School
62	Region Vocational0 Vocational HS, ME	Vocational
72	Richard J. Kinsella Magnet School of Performing Arts, CT	Magnet
141	Ridge HS, NJ	Award Winning School
142	Rock Creek Junior/Senior HS, KS	Award Winning School
49	Rutland Senior High School, VT	Public High School
99	Servite HS, CA	Parochial
50	South High School, ND	Public High School
100	St. Mary's HS, MO	Parochial
145	Thomas Jefferson High School for Science and Technology, VA	Award Winning School
38	Timberlane Middle School, NH	Public Middle School
29	Tombaugh Elementary School, NM	Public Elementary School
101	Totino-Grace HS, MN	Parochial
39	Tremont Middle School, IL	Public Middle School
146	Trion HS, GA	Award Winning School
126	The Urban School of San Francisco, CA	Apple Distinguished School

Page #	School Name	School Type
147	Vestavia HS, AL	Award Winning School
109	Waldorf School of Princeton, NJ	Waldorf
73	Waterbury Arts Magnet School, CT	Magnet
148	West Lyon HS, IA	Award Winning School
128	Westside HS, NE	Apple Distinguished School
40	Westwood Middle School, WV	Public Middle School
41	Windham Middle School, NH	Public Middle School

Cognitive Development

After emotional development, cognitive and academic development of students is the second-most frequently occurring theme in American school mission statements. Again, we have observed many different ways schools choose to invoke the theme of cognitive development in their mission statement. In general, schools incorporate cognitive development in their mission statements using four distinct approaches:

1. Knowledge and Skills
2. Academic Attitude
3. Academic Achievement
4. Academic Curriculum

Knowledge and Skills

The first way schools invoke the cognitive development theme in their mission statements emphasizes the school's role in developing specific knowledge and skills in their students. These skills can relate to basic academic skills or to higher-order skills such as critical thinking, creativity, and leadership. The mission statement of Leo Junior/Senior High School in Indiana provides a rather straightforward example from this category:

> Our mission is students distinguished by achievement, knowledge, skills and character.
>
> —Leo Junior/Senior High School
> Leo, Indiana (Award Winning School, p. 137)

The mission of the Pierson Vocational High School in Nogales, Arizona, provides a second example that articulates a more specific set of skills that is at the core of the school's mission:

> Pierson Vocational High School's Philosophy is to inspire all students to develop marketable 21st century skills. These skills include reading, writing, mathematics, computer knowledge, collaboration and the integrity of being a responsible and productive citizen.
>
> Pierson Vocational High School
> Nogales, Arizona (Vocational School, p. 60)

The following are examples of the language that different school mission statements use in relation to the development of knowledge and skills:

- Help students to build knowledge and skills
- Help students develop communication skills
- Develop children who are problem solvers
- Develop in students the intellectual skills and habits necessary to succeed in competitive high schools, colleges, and the world beyond
- Equip students with skills in technology, problem solving, and critical thinking
- Promote the development of technological skills
- Provide a knowledge-based education
- Provide students with practical knowledge
- Foster achievement, knowledge, and skills

Academic Attitude

A second way we have seen schools include cognitive development in their mission statements relates to the development of academic attitudes in students. For this category, developing specific knowledge or skills are not the target, but rather fostering an intellectual curiosity and a particular type of intellectual attitude in their students. The mission statement of the Normal Park Museum Magnet in Chattanooga, Tennessee provides a good example from this subcategory:

> To instill lifelong intellectual curiosity, sound judgment and deep understanding by building a solid educational foundation based

on meaningful exploration and discovery. We shall accomplish this through collaborative partnerships with parents, museums, and the community in a unique, creative and dynamic environment.

—Normal Park Museum Magne
Chattanooga, Tennessee (Magnet School, p. 71)

Common expressions and excerpts from school mission statements describing academic attitude follow:

- Challenge students to maximize their growth intellectually
- Challenge students to broaden their minds
- Develop talents and abilities
- Develop independent thinkers
- Develop creative and adaptable individuals
- Develop clear thinkers
- Develop flexible thinkers
- Develop students with the courage to initiate change
- Develop articulate students
- Foster intellectual clarity
- Foster excellence in learning
- Foster artistic, independent, and critical thinking
- Foster a respect for both academic and artistic excellence
- Understand the intellectual needs of students
- Instill intellectual curiosity, sound judgment, and deep understanding

Academic Achievement

A third way schools describe cognitive development in their mission statements is to speak distinctly of specific academic achievement goals. The typical emphasis here is on students demonstrating their proficiency via test scores or other academic achievements. Emphasizing standardized test score results as a central part of their school mission statement, Nature Coast Technical High School in Brooksville, Florida, provides one example:

Nature Coast Technical High School's mission is to equip students with skills in technology, problem solving, critical thinking and social interactions by developing an atmosphere of trust, high expectations and consistent support. Our success will be measured through student achievement of maximum potential; parental, community, and employer satisfaction with our students; and improvement on standardized tests such as the FCAT, ACT and SAT.

—Nature Coast Technical High School
Brooksville, Florida (Vocational School, p. 56)

Common expressions and excerpts from school mission statements describing academic achievement follow:

- ◆ Provide a strong academic curriculum
- ◆ Provide an education that allows students the opportunity to be accepted to a four-year university, a community college, or a certificate program in a high-wage, high-demand technical area
- ◆ Focus on high academic achievement
- ◆ Focus on rigorous academic standards
- ◆ Emphasize intellectual achievement along with imaginative, artistic, and moral growth of students
- ◆ Our success will be measured by improvement on standardized tests such as the SAT and ACT
- ◆ Our students will meet or exceed state standards

Academic Curriculum

A final aspect of cognitive development we have seen emphasized in mission statements relates to specific curricular issues. The focus here is typically on the input side (i.e., what the school offers students) rather than the output (i.e., what the students will produce or possess). The mission statement of Nuweetooun School in Exeter, Rhode Island, provides an example of curricular input focus:

The mission of this school is to educate all students in a respectful, stimulating, and engaging environment. Our program integrates core educational curriculum standards in Language Arts, Mathematics, Science, Social Studies, and Health with a concentration on Environmental Education and Native Culture and History.

We are committed to creating an experiential, integrated, and collaborative learning environment in which to develop well-rounded, enthusiastic, and self-motivated learners. Our students experience education that embraces their learning styles, honors their multiple intelligences, and enriches their educational, social, spiritual, and cultural development in order to develop the whole person.

—Nuweetooun School
Exeter, Rhode Island (Native American/Tribal School, p. 90)

The following are examples of the language that different school mission statements use in relation to academic curricula:

- ◆ Provide a technology-infused integrated curriculum that demands academic excellence
- ◆ Provide a curriculum that integrates the academic, artistic, and practical
- ◆ Promote academic rigor

Schools including the Cognitive Development theme in their mission statements:

Page #	School Name	School Type
103	Academe of the Oaks, GA	Waldorf
76	Academy for Business and Leadership, FL	Charter
67	Advanced Technologies Academy, NV	Magnet
93	Archmere Academy, DE	Parochial
112	Austin Montessori School, TX	Montessori
130	BASIS, AZ	Award Winning School
108	The Bay School, ME	Waldorf
44	Bellows Free Academy, VT	Public High School
46	Bossier High School, LA	Public High School
94	Brophy College Prep, AZ	Parochial
95	Cardinal Newman School, SC	Parochial
68	Carter Academy, TX	Magnet
131	Chapin HS, SC	Award Winning School
114	Chesterfield Montessori School, MO	Montessori
132	Columbiana HS, OH	Award Winning School
77	Community Roots Charter School, NY	Charter
78	Compass Charter School, ID	Charter
120	Del Mar Middle School, CA	Apple Distinguished School
104	Desert Marigold School, AZ	Waldorf
133	Devine HS, TX	Award Winning School
35	Dr. Martin Luther King, Jr. Middle School, MD	Public Middle School
106	Emerson Waldorf School, NC	Waldorf
96	Father Gabriel Richard Catholic HS, MI	Parochial
69	Forest Lake Elementary School, SC	Magnet

Page #	School Name	School Type
87	Gila Crossing Community School, AZ	Native American
79	Harding Fine Arts Academy, OK	Charter
33	Henry J. McLaughlin Jr. Middle School, NH	Public Middle School
135	Hingham High School, MA	Award Winning School
107	Honolulu Waldorf School, HI	Waldorf
123	Howard Elementary School, OR	Apple Distinguished School
25	Jerome Stamply Elementary School, MS	Public Elementary School
97	Jesuit HS, OR	Parochial
80	Jumoke Academy Charter School, CT	Charter
88	Kayenta Middle School, AZ	Native American
81	KIPP Academy of Opportunity, CA	Charter
82	KIPP Sunshine Peak Academy, CO	Charter
137	Leo Junior/Senior HS, IN	Award Winning School
124	Lilla G. Frederick Pilot Middle School, MA	Apple Distinguished School
138	Middle College HS, CA	Award Winning School
98	Montgomery Catholic Prep, AL	Parochial
56	Nature Coast Technical HS, FL	Vocational
89	Nay Ah Shing School, MN	Native American
57	North County Trade Tech School, CA	Vocational
90	Nuweetooun School, RI	Native American
58	Oakland Technical HS, CA	Vocational
117	Pacific Rim International School, CA	Montessori
27	Parkside Elementary, WY	Public Elementary School
59	Paul M. Hodgson Vocational Tech HS, DE	Vocational
60	Pierson Vocational HS, AZ	Vocational
139	Preuss UCSD, CA	Award Winning School
36	Princeton Middle School, WV	Public Middle School
61	Queens Vocational and Technical HS, NY	Vocational
72	Richard J. Kinsella Magnet School of Performing Arts, CT	Magnet
141	Ridge HS, NJ	Award Winning School
83	Rilke Schule German School of Arts & Sciences, AK	Charter
49	Rutland Senior High School, VT	Public High School
143	School of Science and Engineering, TX	Award Winning School

Page #	School Name	School Type
125	Science Leadership Academy, PA	Apple Distinguished School
144	School for the Talented and Gifted, TX	Award Winning School
99	Servite HS, CA	Parochial
50	South High School, ND	Public High School
38	Timberlane Middle School, NH	Public Middle School
101	Totino-Grace HS, MN	Parochial
146	Trion HS, GA	Award Winning School
109	Waldorf School of Princeton, NJ	Waldorf
110	Waldorf School on the Roaring Fork, CO	Waldorf
127	Washington Middle School, WI	Apple Distinguished School
73	Waterbury Arts Magnet School, CT	Magnet
41	Windham Middle School, NH	Public Middle School

Challenging Environment

The idea of the school as a "challenging environment" was frequently invoked across the American school mission statements we examined. Across all school types, we found that schools invoked the message or theme of "challenging environment" in their mission statements using three distinct approaches:

1. Expectations of Students
2. Instructional Elements
3. Environmental Elements

Expectations of Students

One of the ways we have observed schools invoke a challenging environment in their mission statements relates to the expectations that are set out for students. Many schools' mission statements expressly address the importance of setting high standards for students and helping students to maximize their potential. In addition, school mission statements in this category often invoke the importance of providing a well-rounded education. The mission statement of Lakeville North High School in Minnesota provides an example that captures many of these components:

Lakeville North High School is committed to creating a community that instills integrity and challenges students to reach their individual potential.

—Lakeville North High School
Lakeville, Minnesota (Award Winning School, p. 136)

Common expressions and excerpts from school mission statements describing expectations of students follow:

- Promote high expectations for all
- Foster an atmosphere of high expectations
- Hold high expectations for all students during challenging instruction
- Challenge students to maximize their educational abilities
- Challenge students to maximize their growth emotionally, socially, and intellectually
- Provide a curriculum that integrates academic, physical, experiential, and artistic work
- Provide future generations with an education that will meet their needs in a constantly changing world
- Teach children to see the connections between school and the world
- Assist each student in the full development of his gifts and talents through a challenging college preparatory academic program, athletic endeavors, and a well-rounded program of extracurricular activities

Instructional Elements

A second way schools invoke a challenging environment theme in their mission statements relates to instructional elements and issues. School mission statements here focus on instructional aspects such as standards-based instruction, differentiated instruction, innovative instructional strategies, and engaging educational activities. The mission statement of Timberlane Regional Middle School in Plaistow, New Hampshire, provides an example that indicates its emphasis on a standards-based curriculum and differentiated instruction:

The Timberlane Regional Middle School is committed to sustaining a collaborative learning environment so that our students may become successful, independent learners. It is our mission to:

- ◆ Provide a safe, respectful, and nurturing environment that encourages enthusiasm for learning.
- ◆ Foster responsible citizenship and provide opportunities for students to acquire and demonstrate leadership and service.
- ◆ Provide a challenging, integrated, standards-based curriculum.
- ◆ Meet the individual needs of students by identifying differences and using assessment to differentiate instruction and learning.

—Timberlane Regional Middle School
Plaistow, New Hampshire (Public Middle School, p. 38)

As a second example of instructional elements in a school mission statement, Tremont Middle School in Illinois provides an example that does not mention curriculum standards, per se, but still focuses on providing their students challenging and engaging activities:

The mission of Tremont Middle School is to provide a positive environment incorporating meaningful and challenging activities designed to instill a desire for life long learning.

—Tremont Middle School
Tremont, Illinois (Public Middle School, p. 39)

The following are examples of the language that different school mission statements use in relation to the instructional elements:

- ◆ Provide a rigorous education
- ◆ Provide a challenging, integrated, standards-based curriculum
- ◆ Provide a developmentally appropriate curriculum and enriched extended day activities
- ◆ Provide differentiated education
- ◆ Provide remedial assistance for students needing basic skill support
- ◆ Implement research-based instruction
- ◆ Integrate core curriculum standards
- ◆ Incorporate 21st century teaching skills
- ◆ Use assessment to differentiate instruction
- ◆ Recognize individual differences and abilities
- ◆ Incorporate meaningful and challenging activities
- ◆ Foster a culture of innovation based on ethical behavior and the shared interests of humanity
- ◆ Encourage innovative teaching strategies that emphasize enjoyable and relevant educational experiences

◆ Educate children in a respectful, stimulating, and engaging environment

Environmental Elements

The final approach to describing a challenging environment we have found across school mission statements relates to different environmental elements in a school that provide students a challenging environment. Again, the focus here is on the input side of the education—what is the school attempting to do to create a challenging environment? The mission statement from the Ridge High School in Basking Ridge, New Jersey, provides an example that illustrates this approach:

> The mission of Ridge High School is to prepare each student to be a knowledgeable and reputable member of society who functions with self-esteem, discipline, integrity, and compassion. In support of this mission, the faculty and administration are committed to:
>
> ◆ creating an orderly environment for students characterized by high expectations, respect for both academic and artistic excellence, personal achievement, and mutual respect.
> ◆ providing a strong academic program in all education areas.
> ◆ providing quality instruction in all classes.
> ◆ providing remedial assistance for students needing basic skill support.
> ◆ assisting each prospective graduate to enter college, advanced training, or the work force.
> ◆ maintaining close contact with parents and community.
> ◆ creating an environment for faculty characterized by collegiality, collaboration, inquiry, and respect for the knowledge base of the profession.
>
> —Ridge High School
> Basking Ridge, New Jersey (Award Winning School, p. 141)

Common expressions and excerpts describing environmental elements from American school mission statements follow:

◆ Provide an enriched environment
◆ Create challenging opportunities to educate students in an atmosphere of trust and mutual respect

- ◆ Create an environment that prepares students to be life-long learners
- ◆ Students learn in a project-based environment
- ◆ Our goal is for students to be successful in college and beyond

Schools including the Challenging Environment theme in their mission statements:

Page #	School Name	School Type
66	Academic Magnet HS, SC	Magnet
76	Academy for Business and Leadership, FL	Charter
45	Billings West High School, MT	Public High School
95	Cardinal Newman School, SC	Parochial
131	Chapin HS, SC	Award Winning School
86	Chief Leschi School, WA	Native American
133	Devine HS, TX	Award Winning School
122	Empire HS, AZ	Apple Distinguished School
47	Hellgate High School, MT	Public High School
33	Henry J. McLaughlin Jr. Middle School, NH	Public Middle School
135	Hingham High School, MA	Award Winning School
80	Jumoke Academy Charter School, CT	Charter
136	Lakeville North HS, MN	Award Winning School
124	Lilla G. Frederick Pilot Middle School, MA	Apple Distinguished School
138	Middle College HS, CA	Award Winning School
56	Nature Coast Technical HS, FL	Vocational
90	Nuweetooun School, RI	Native American
36	Princeton Middle School, WV	Public Middle School
72	Richard J. Kinsella Magnet School of Performing Arts, CT	Magnet
141	Ridge HS, NJ	Award Winning School
142	Rock Creek Junior/Senior HS, KS	Award Winning School
143	School of Science and Engineering, TX	Award Winning School
99	Servite HS, CA	Parochial
100	St. Mary's HS, MO	Parochial
145	Thomas Jefferson High School for Science and Technology, VA	Award Winning School
38	Timberlane Middle School, NH	Public Middle School
29	Tombaugh Elementary School, NM	Public Elementary School
39	Tremont Middle School, IL	Public Middle School

Page #	School Name	School Type
147	Vestavia HS, AL	Award Winning School
127	Washington Middle School, WI	Apple Distinguished School
73	Waterbury Arts Magnet School, CT	Magnet
52	Wynne High School, AR	Public High School

Safe/Nurturing Environment

Across all levels and types of American schools, many mission statements include information about the school being a safe and nurturing environment for students. Overall, we have found that schools express their safe/nurturing environment in three different ways:

1. Safe Environment
2. Nurturing Environment
3. Specific Components of a Nurturing Environment

Safe Environment

The first way schools invoke a safe/nurturing environment theme in their mission statements relates to the provision of a safe educational environment. In Morgantown, West Virginia, the Westwood Middle School mission statement speaks to the safe environment the school is cultivating:

> The staff of Westwood Middle School will provide a safe, equitable learning environment that will strive for the success of all of our students. We believe that by creating and continuing this positive atmosphere, we will be promoting one's self worth and accomplishments while providing high expectations for all. This atmosphere will also enhance a positive attitude toward school and school-community involvement.
>
> —Westwood Middle School
> Morgantown, West Virginia (Public Middle School, p. 40)

We have found that the majority of schools that include a reference to safe environment also include a reference to a nurturing environment in their mission statements. The Paul M. Hodgson Vocational Technical High School in Newark, Delaware, provides a prototypical example:

Our mission is to prepare students vocationally and academically to be productive, employable citizens of society by integrating high quality instruction and technology in a safe, caring, and cooperative school environment.

> —Paul M. Hodgson Vocational Technical High School
> Newark, Delaware (Vocational School, p. 59)

Common expressions and excerpts from school mission statements describing a safe environment follow:

- ◆ Provide a safe learning environment
- ◆ Provide a safe, equitable learning environment
- ◆ Provide safe, respectful, and nurturing environment
- ◆ Provide a secure educational setting
- ◆ Provide a safe, nurturing environment for the growth and development of young children
- ◆ Provide a safe and nurturing environment while providing high-quality instruction
- ◆ Provide safe, orderly, and healthy environment
- ◆ Provide a peaceful, safe, and clean environment
- ◆ Provide a safe, caring, and cooperative environment

Nurturing Environment

As previously stated, the nurturing environment theme was included in many mission statements that focus on a safe environment; however, there are some examples that focus primarily on nurturing, such as the Doña Ana Elementary School in Las Cruces, New Mexico:

> Our goal at Doña Ana Elementary is to nurture and empower every student to reach their full potential, giving them many opportunities to adapt to their changing world and instill a love of learning.
> —Doña Ana Elementary School
> Las Cruces, New Mexico (Public Elementary School, p. 23)

The following are examples of the language that different school mission statements use in relation to the development of a nurturing environment:

- ◆ Create a positive environment
- ◆ Nurture and empower every student
- ◆ Provide an encouraging environment

- Provide an education that nurtures the whole child
- Provide a supportive environment

Specific Components of a Nurturing Environment

A third way that school mission statements express a safe/nurturing environment theme concerns the specific components in such an environment. For example, some mission statements focus on creating an atmosphere of trust, respect, and compassion. Others focus on respecting the diversity of the student body. The mission statement of Austin Montessori School in Texas provides a comprehensive example that outlines a number of different components all related to the development of a nurturing school environment:

> The mission of Austin Montessori School is to guide the intellectual and character development of each child along a path towards his full and unknown potential. We strive to cultivate compassion and respect, independence and belonging, and freedom and self-discipline, in rich academic and social environments that are designed for each plane of development and honor the complementary needs of the individual and the group. We value an educational setting that is inclusive and recognizes the authentic nature of the child and nurtures a reverence for the organic order of the universe. Through parent and staff education, we work to develop a school and family culture that preserves and protects a healthy childhood. Our aim is to serve children possessing an ample range of temperaments and a variety of learning styles and rates. At the same time we seek to avoid pathologizing and labeling the normal range of children's behaviors and differences in learning. We are dedicated to Montessori's mission of world peace through human development.
>
> —Austin Montessori School
> Austin, Texas (Montessori School, p. 112)

Common expressions and excerpts from school mission statements describing specific components of a nurturing environment follow:

- Create challenging opportunities to educate students in an atmosphere of trust and mutual respect
- Provide a school climate that values mutual respect and dignity
- Provide a peaceful environment with compassionate staff
- Facilitate learning for all students and promote respect for others
- Foster a collaborative learning environment

- ◆ Cultivate responsible and compassionate shapers of society
- ◆ Meet the needs of students at all levels/abilities
- ◆ Welcome a student body that is economically and culturally diverse
- ◆ Believe that all students have potential
- ◆ Serve children possessing an ample range of temperaments and a variety of learning styles and rates
- ◆ Serve students of all socio-economic backgrounds
- ◆ Our students experience an education that honors their multiple intelligences

Schools including the Safe/Nurturing Environment theme in their mission statements:

Page #	School Name	School Type
76	Academy for Business and Leadership, FL	Charter
112	Austin Montessori School, TX	Montessori
108	The Bay School, ME	Waldorf
149	Bodine HS for International Affairs, PA	Award Winning School
95	Cardinal Newman School, SC	Parochial
114	Chesterfield Montessori School, MO	Montessori
86	Chief Leschi School, WA	Native American
22	DeSoto Central Elementary School, MS	Public Elementary School
23	Doña Ana Elementary School, NM	Public Elementary School
115	Dynamite Montessori, AZ	Montessori
69	Forest Lake Elementary School, SC	Magnet
87	Gila Crossing Community School, AZ	Native American
47	Hellgate High School, MT	Public High School
80	Jumoke Academy Charter School, CT	Charter
88	Kayenta Middle School, AZ	Native American
124	Lilla G. Frederick Pilot Middle School, MA	Apple Distinguished School
56	Nature Coast Technical HS, FL	Vocational
89	Nay Ah Shing School, MN	Native American
58	Oakland Technical HS, CA	Vocational
59	Paul M. Hodgson Vocational Tech HS, DE	Vocational
139	Preuss UCSD, CA	Award Winning School
36	Princeton Middle School, WV	Public Middle School
28	Providence Elementary School, UT	Public Elementary School
49	Rutland Senior High School, VT	Public High School

Page #	School Name	School Type
38	Timberlane Middle School, NH	Public Middle School
29	Tombaugh Elementary School, NM	Public Elementary School
101	Totino-Grace HS, MN	Parochial
39	Tremont Middle School, IL	Public Middle School
73	Waterbury Arts Magnet School, CT	Magnet
40	Westwood Middle School, WV	Public Middle School
41	Windham Middle School, NH	Public Middle School

Civic Development

As we have previously discussed, civic development has been an important component of the school purpose debate for centuries. In our study of school mission statements, we have found that American schools typically invoke civic development in four distinct ways:

1. Responsible Citizens
2. Productive Citizens
3. Leadership
4. Service and Responsibility

Responsible Citizens

One way schools often include a citizenship theme in their mission statements is through the cultivation students as responsible citizens. This phrase is invoked frequently in school mission statements. From our review, responsible citizens are often framed as those students who integrate into and participate in the life of their local communities. To this end, Eastside High School in Gainesville, Florida, provides an excellent example of this type of school mission statement:

> Eastside High School seeks to build community among our highly diverse students and their families, whether they come from different neighborhoods in Gainesville or from countries and cultures around the world. All members of our fluid and lively school family—parents, students, faculty, and support staff—should show respect and encouragement for each other. The mission of Eastside

High School's community is that all students develop the skills and knowledge necessary for them to survive, learn, adapt, and grow—leading to a lifetime pattern of responsible citizenship.

—Eastside High School
Gainesville, Florida (Award Winning School, p. 134)

Common expressions and excerpts from school mission statements describing responsible citizens follow:

◆ Foster responsible citizenship
◆ Develop educated, caring, responsible world citizens
◆ Develop in students a lifetime pattern of responsible citizenship
◆ Develop students who are responsible, contributing citizens of their communities
◆ Prepare students to become knowledgeable and reputable members of society

Productive Citizens

A second way schools categorize a citizenship theme in their mission statements involves the cultivation of students into productive citizens, or productivity in general. This focus on productivity is often connected to the notion of future employment in the job sector, but we have observed examples that also imply a notion of civic productivity. The mission statement of Chapin High School in South Carolina provides an example:

The mission of Chapin High School of Lexington Richland School District Five, in partnership with the community, is to provide challenging curricula with high expectations for learning that develop productive citizens who can solve problems and contribute to a global society.

—Chapin High School
Chapin, South Carolina (Award Winning School, p. 131)

The following are examples of the language that different school mission statements use in relation to the development of productive citizens:

◆ Develop employable citizens
◆ Develop productive citizens in a multicultural, changing society

◆ Prepare students to enter the workforce or pursue post-secondary education as civic-minded adults

Leadership

The third way we have found that schools include a citizenship component in their mission statements relates to the notion of developing future leaders. Although leadership itself does not always imply civic leadership, many schools expressly invoke the importance of developing the next generation of the country's leaders. The mission statement of Trion High School in Georgia provides an example focusing on leadership:

> To promote personal growth and leadership development through family and consumer sciences education. Focusing on the multiple roles of family member, wage earner, and community leader, members develop skills for life through—
>
> ◆ character development,
> ◆ creative and critical thinking;
> ◆ interpersonal communication;
> ◆ practical knowledge; and
> ◆ vocational preparation
>
> —Trion High School
> Trion, Georgia (Award Winning School, p. 146)

Common expressions and excerpts from school mission statements describing leadership follow:

◆ Develop global leaders
◆ Develop responsible leaders for the 21st century

Service and Responsibility

A fourth aspect of the citizenship theme found across the school mission statements relates to service and responsibility. This notion is found in a number of different statements and is especially prevalent in the parochial school mission statements. The mission statement of Vestavia Hills High School in Alabama speaks to the importance of community service:

The mission of Vestavia Hills High School, a collaborative learning community with a continuing tradition of excellence, is to cultivate responsible and compassionate shapers of society by fostering personal growth through community service, charter development, and a rigorous, varied, relevant curriculum.

—Vestavia Hills High School
Vestavia Hills, Alabama (Award Winning School, p. 147)

Common expressions and excerpts from school mission statements describing service and responsibility follow:

◆ Promote social responsibility
◆ Encourage community service
◆ Instill a dedication to service

Schools including the Civic Development theme in their mission statements:

Page #	School Name	School Type
76	Academy for Business and Leadership, FL	Charter
93	Archmere Academy, DE	Parochial
43	Bentonville High School, AR	Public High School
44	Bellows Free Academy, VT	Public High School
45	Billings West High School, MT	Public High School
131	Chapin HS, SC	Award Winning School
86	Chief Leschi School, WA	Native American
22	DeSoto Central Elementary School, MS	Public Elementary School
134	Eastside HS, FL	Award Winning School
121	Echo Lake ES, WA	Apple Distinguished School
106	Emerson Waldorf School, NC	Waldorf
96	Father Gabriel Richard Catholic HS, MI	Parochial
69	Forest Lake Elementary School, SC	Magnet
33	Henry J. McLaughlin Jr. Middle School, NH	Public Middle School
135	Hingham High School, MA	Award Winning School
97	Jesuit HS, OR	Parochial
136	Lakeville North HS, MN	Award Winning School
89	Nay Ah Shing School, MN	Native American
59	Paul M. Hodgson Vocational Tech HS, DE	Vocational
60	Pierson Vocational HS, AZ	Vocational
139	Preuss UCSD, CA	Award Winning School

Page #	School Name	School Type
61	Queens Vocational and Technical HS, NY	Vocational
141	Ridge HS, NJ	Award Winning School
49	Rutland Senior High School, VT	Public High School
99	Servite HS, CA	Parochial
38	Timberlane Middle School, NH	Public Middle School
147	Vestavia HS, AL	Award Winning School
73	Waterbury Arts Magnet School, CT	Magnet
51	Winooski High School, VT	Public High School

Integration Into Local Community

Across our research, we have identified three complementary ways that schools integrate concepts of local community and community integration into their mission statements:

1. Students Contributing to the Community
2. Community Working Together
3. Community Focused on Developing Responsible Students

Students Contributing to Community

The first way that school mission statements can invoke a local community theme portrays how students are expected to contribute to their local communities. This can take the form of participating in the political structure, the religious community, or some other elements of the local community, including the workplace. The mission statement of Servite High School in Anaheim, California, provides a clear example from this school invokes local community. The emphasis here is on ensuring that students at the school are active participants within their local communities:

> To provide a multifaceted and holistic educational experience which prepares students for post-secondary studies and responsible participation in the church and civic communities. To achieve excellence in a well-ordered and disciplined environment permeated by the Servite tradition of fraternity, service, and Marian spirituality. To assist each student in the full development of his gifts and talents through a challenging college preparatory academic program, athletic

endeavors, and a well-rounded program of extracurricular activities. To be a lived-faith community that awakens students and faculty to an inquiry into the meaning of their spiritual lives through religious studies, shared worship, campus ministry, and Christian service programs. To respect the dignity and rights of all faculty and student body members. To make our decisions in the spirit of the gospel of Jesus Christ and in accord with the collegial tradition of the order of friar servants of Mary.

—Servite High School
Anaheim, California (Parochial School, p. 99)

Common expressions and excerpts from school mission statements describing students contributing to the community follow:

◆ Develop in students the life skills needed to succeed in their own lives and contribute to the well-being of their communities
◆ Prepare students for responsible participation in the church and civic communities

Community Working Together

A second way schools invoke their local communities in their mission statement focuses on the relationship between the community and the school. Here, the focus of the mission statements is not necessarily on the students' contribution to the community, but rather an emphasis on a partnership that requires the involvement of the community in the school. The mission statement of the Middle College High School in Santa Ana, California, provides one example from this subcategory, highlighting the collaboration between the local university system and the local school district:

The mission of Middle College High School, a collaborative between the Santa Ana Unified School District and Santa Ana College, is to provide a supportive, academically challenging environment for underserved youth with high academic potential that leads not only to a rich high school education but also leads to independence and success in college and beyond.

—Middle College High School
Santa Ana, California (Award Winning School, p. 138)

The following are examples of the language that different school mission statements use to describe the community working together:

♦ Create a community committed to working together
♦ Develop a sense of community
♦ Develop a community where all involved in the students' formation collaborate to create a climate of cooperation, respect, openness, and trust
♦ Foster a strong sense of community
♦ Empower students, staff, and parents to learn, work, and grow together
♦ Affirm that education is a partnership between students, parents, educators, and the community
♦ Work cooperatively with parents in addressing individual needs and differences
♦ Through guidance, we will get there together
♦ Through parent and staff education, we work to develop a school and family culture that preserves and protects a healthy childhood
♦ The values of the school create a community of children, alumni, parents, and faculty imbued with reverence for others and the natural world
♦ We have a tradition of committed faculty, alumni, families, and friends
♦ We are an environment that expects family involvement
♦ Our program will be characterized by the cooperative presence and unified support of families, businesses, and educational and civic groups with whom our students will interact

Community Focused on Developing Responsible Students

A third way that schools express the integration into local community in their mission statements is by highlighting the role of community in student development. Here, the emphasis is on what the community can do to help foster student development. Note the contrast to past examples that emphasized what students can provide for the community or the equal partnership between the community and the school. The mission statement of West Lyon High School in Inwood, Iowa, emphasizes this role of local community:

West Lyon School is committed to the service of the students entrusted to us. We strive for the fullest development and maturation of each child. We also recognize that the school is not the only institution that plays a vital role in the growth of young people. The home, church, law enforcement agencies, and social welfare institutions also have a major responsibility.

—West Lyon High School
Inwood, Iowa (Award Winning School, p. 148)

Schools referencing the Local Community theme in their mission statements:

Page #	School Name	School Type
76	Academy for Business and Leadership, FL	Charter
108	The Bay School, ME	Waldorf
46	Bossier High School, LA	Public High School
131	Chapin HS, SC	Award Winning School
86	Chief Leschi School, WA	Native American
134	Eastside HS, FL	Award Winning School
69	Forest Lake Elementary School, SC	Magnet
32	Glen Crest Middle School, IL	Public Middle School
47	Hellgate High School, MT	Public High School
33	Henry J. McLaughlin Jr. Middle School, NH	Public Middle School
135	Hingham High School, MA	Award Winning School
124	Lilla G. Frederick Pilot Middle School, MA	Apple Distinguished School
35	Dr. Martin Luther King, Jr. Middle School, MD	Public Middle School
48	Montpelier High School, VT	Public High School
89	Nay Ah Shing School, MN	Native American
71	Normal Park Museum Magnet, TN	Magnet
27	Parkside Elementary, WY	Public Elementary School
139	Preuss UCSD, CA	Award Winning School
141	Ridge HS, NJ	Award Winning School
49	Rutland Senior High School, VT	Public High School
50	South High School, ND	Public High School
29	Tombaugh Elementary School, NM	Public Elementary School
146	Trion HS, GA	Award Winning School
73	Waterbury Arts Magnet School, CT	Magnet
148	West Lyon HS, IA	Award Winning School
40	Westwood Middle School, WV	Public Middle School

Integration Into Global Community

In addition to some schools' emphasis on local community integration, numerous school mission statements focus on the importance of developing students who are able to integrate into the global community. Although frequently related to the civic development theme, many school mission statements focus on a distinctly global perspective. Across the mission statements that emphasize this global perspective, we observe four different approaches:

1. Adapt to a Changing World
2. Develop Global Leaders
3. Prepare Globally Responsible Citizens
4. Prepare for Global Competition

Adapt to a Changing World

One way schools evoke a global worldview in their mission statements is by describing their aim of helping students to adapt to a changing world. The Sioux Valley Middle School in Volga, South Dakota, provides a succinct example:

> Preparing individuals to succeed in an ever-changing global community.
>
> —Sioux Valley Middle School
> Volga, South Dakota (Public Middle School, p. 37)

Common expressions and excerpts from school mission statements that describe adapting to a changing world include:

- Adapt to their changing world
- Grow together in an ever-changing world
- Prepare individuals to succeed in an ever-changing global community

Develop Global Leaders

A second way schools express integration into the global community in their mission statements focuses on the development of global leaders. Mission statements in this category express the expectations that school will both prepare students for a global future and be its leaders. The mission statement of A.B. Combs Elementary in Raleigh, North Carolina, provides a succinct example:

> To develop global leaders one child at a time.
> —A. B. Combs Elementary
> Raleigh, North Carolina (Magnet School, p. 65)

The following are examples of the language that different school mission statements use to describe the development of global leaders:

- Develop global leaders
- Inspire leaders who are devoted to the service of others in a global community
- Motivate students to contribute to their local, national, and world communities

Prepare Globally Responsible Citizens

A third approach that schools use to evoke the global community theme relates to the development of globally responsible citizens. Unlike the citizenship theme observed more commonly in mission statements, many schools' mission statements have a distinct global emphasis. The mission statement of Academic Magnet High School in North Charleston, South Carolina provides an example:

> The mission of the Academic Magnet High School is to challenge each student, teacher and parent with the high expectations of a rigorous curriculum. We provide a learning environment that thoroughly prepares students for college and develops their self-esteem. Our students are encouraged to be citizens of the world, to acquire a sense of global responsibility, and to cultivate a respect for cultural diversity.
> —Academic Magnet High School
> North Charleston, South Carolina (Magnet School, p. 66)

Common expressions and excerpts from school mission statements emphasizing responsible global citizenship include:

- Develop educated, caring, responsible world citizens

+ Develop students who understand their moral obligation to the global community
+ Promote responsibility to the world community
+ Our students are encouraged to be citizens of the world, to acquire a sense of global responsibility, and to cultivate a respect for cultural diversity

Prepare for Global Competition

A final approach that schools take when discussing global integration in their mission statements is preparing students for a competitive global environment. In these mission statements, schools portray themselves as preparing students for a future that is both competitive and beyond US borders. The mission statement of the Jumoke Academy Charter School in Hartford, Connecticut, provides a prototypical example:

> The mission of Jumoke Academy Charter School is to prepare children to successfully compete in the global marketplace despite the social and economic challenges they may presently face. The academy is dedicated to rigorous academic and social standards achieved by holding high expectations for all students during challenging instruction.
>
> The concept of "Jumoke" is central to the academy' s mission to provide a safe and nurturing environment for its children while providing high quality instruction. Students in Pk–8th grade will be offered a developmentally appropriate curriculum and an enriched program of extended day activities which addresses the unique talents and background of each child in the areas of science, mathematics, language arts, technology, physical education, music and art enrichment.
>
> —Jumoke Academy Charter School
> Hartford, Connecticut (Charter School, p. 80)

The following are examples of the language that different school mission statements use to describe the process of preparing students for global competition:

+ Prepare children to successfully compete in the global marketplace
+ Compete successfully in a changing world

Schools referencing the Global Community theme in their mission statements:

Page #	School Name	School Type
65	A.B. Combs Elementary, NC	Magnet
103	Academe of the Oaks, GA	Waldorf
66	Academic Magnet HS, SC	Magnet
76	Academy for Business and Leadership, FL	Charter
93	Archmere Academy, DE	Parochial
112	Austin Montessori School, TX	Montessori
43	Bentonville High School, AR	Public High School
94	Brophy College Prep, AZ	Parochial
131	Chapin HS, SC	Award Winning School
86	Chief Leschi School, WA	Native American
77	Community Roots Charter School, NY	Charter
104	DeSoto Central Elementary School, MS	Public Elementary School
23	Doña Ana Elementary School, NM	Public Elementary School
106	Emerson Waldorf School, NC	Waldorf
33	Henry J. McLaughlin Jr. Middle School, NH	Public Middle School
135	Hingham High School, MA	Award Winning School
107	Honolulu Waldorf School, HI	Waldorf
80	Jumoke Academy Charter School, CT	Charter
136	Lakeville North HS, MN	Award Winning School
48	Montpelier High School, VT	Public High School
117	Pacific Rim International School, CA	Montessori
72	Richard J. Kinsella Magnet School of Performing Arts, CT	Magnet
37	Sioux Valley Middle School, SD	Public Middle School
145	Thomas Jefferson High School for Science and Technology, VA	Award Winning School
101	Totino-Grace HS, MN	Parochial

Social Development

Across our research studies, we have generally encountered few schools that emphasize a social development theme in their mission statements. When school mission statements do include a social development strand in the mission statements, they use one of two general approaches:

1. Social Skills
2. Social Attitudes

Social Skills

The first way that schools incorporate social development into their mission statement is by describing the school's role in developing specific social skills in their students. These skills often take the form of interpersonal communication skills, practical knowledge, and teamwork. The mission statement of Queens Vocational and Technical High School in New York City provides an example from this theme:

> Queens Vocational & Technical High School is committed to preparing our students with the critical thinking, problem solving and team building skills necessary to meet the demands of a highly technical and ever expanding global economy. Our dual mission is to graduate students who are not only ready for post-secondary education, but who can also readily integrate into our work force as skilled, productive, contributing citizens. Our students are prepared to succeed.
> —Queens Vocational and Technical High School
> Queens, New York (Vocational School, p. 61)

The following are examples of the language that different school mission statements use to describe the development of social skills:

- Equip students with skills in social interaction
- Provide opportunities for students to demonstrate leadership and service
- Develop students with strong interpersonal communication skills
- Cultivate the innate leadership and creative impulses within all children
- Our students will be able to work with a diverse group of learners
- Promote respect for others
- Develop students who work cooperatively and communicate respectfully
- Develop students with the ability to work with each other in a global context

- ◆ Prepare our students with team building skills
- ◆ Promote teamwork

Social Attitudes

A second way that social development is incorporated into school mission statements relates to the development of specific social attitudes. The emphasis here is not on a specific set of skills, but rather on the development of students as social beings. Within this context, the importance of helping students develop friendships and personal connections with others is typically stressed. The mission statement of Carter Academy in Houston, Texas, illustrates an emphasis on social attitudes:

> We will collaborate as a school community to provide the best instruction for every student in order to meet and exceed grade level expectations regardless of previous academic performance. It is our purpose and responsibility to educate all students to high levels of academic, social, and creative performance while fostering positive growth in social behaviors and attitudes.
>
> —Carter Academy
> Houston, Texas (Magnet School, p. 68)

Common expressions and excerpts from school mission statements describing social attitudes follow:

- ◆ Challenge students to maximize their growth socially
- ◆ Ours is a place where lifelong friendships are formed
- ◆ Promote a sense of belonging
- ◆ Understand the social needs of students

Schools referencing the Social Development theme in their mission statements:

Page #	School Name	School Type
103	Academe of the Oaks, GA	Waldorf
93	Archmere Academy, DE	Parochial
112	Austin Montessori School, TX	Montessori
44	Bellows Free Academy, VT	Public High School
68	Carter Academy, TX	Magnet
115	Dynamite Montessori, AZ	Montessori
69	Forest Lake Elementary School, SC	Magnet

Page #	School Name	School Type
33	Henry J. McLaughlin Jr. Middle School, NH	Public Middle School
135	Hingham High School, MA	Award Winning School
80	Jumoke Academy Charter School, CT	Charter
88	Kayenta Middle School, AZ	Native American
81	KIPP Academy of Opportunity, CA	Charter
56	Nature Coast Technical HS, FL	Vocational
89	Nay Ah Shing School, MN	Native American
90	Nuweetooun School, RI	Native American
58	Oakland Technical HS, CA	Vocational
61	Queens Vocational and Technical HS, NY	Vocational
49	Rutland Senior High School, VT	Public High School
125	Science Leadership Academy, PA	Apple Distinguished School
99	Servite HS, CA	Parochial
50	South High School, ND	Public High School
146	Trion HS, GA	Award Winning School
41	Windham Middle School, NH	Public Middle School

Vocational Preparation

The vocational development theme was common in most vocational/career/technical education schools; however, we have observed school mission statements from various school types that also stressed the importance of vocational themes. Overall, we see three distinct aspects of vocational preparation presented across American school mission statements:

1. Vocational Skills
2. Focus on Job Preparation
3. Response to External Indicators

Vocational Skills

The first way that school mission statements express the theme of vocational development is by emphasizing the importance of equipping students with a particular set of skills. The mission statement of Pierson Vocational

High School in Nogales, Arizona, provides a prototypical example within this subcategory:

> Pierson Vocational High School's Philosophy is to inspire all students to develop marketable 21st century skills. These skills include reading, writing, mathematics, computer knowledge, collaboration and the integrity of being a responsible and productive citizen.
> —Pierson Vocational High School
> Nogales, Arizona (Vocational School, p. 60)

Common expressions and excerpts from school mission statements describing vocational skills follow:

- ◆ Inspire students to develop marketable 21st-century skills
- ◆ Equip students with a strong blend of academic and workforce competencies
- ◆ Teach students technical skills
- ◆ Students will acquire marketable skills
- ◆ Students will graduate with strong vocational skills

Focus on Job Preparation

A second aspect of vocational preparation that many schools express in their mission statements relates to job preparation. Most schools that emphasize vocational preparation are specifically concerned with helping their students develop marketable skills that will help them integrate seamlessly into the workforce. Though not a vocational school, the mission statement of Devine High School in Texas provides an example that emphasizes job preparation:

> The staff of Devine High School believes that each student has the ability to learn. In order for each student to achieve his or her goals in academic and/or vocational development, our mission will be to meet student needs at all levels, motivating and encouraging each student regardless of his or her academic level, socioeconomic status, race, or gender. Upon completion of our mission, each student should be able to make a smooth transition to college, trade or vocational school, military service, or the workplace.
> —Devine High School
> Devine, Texas (Award Winning School, p. 133)

The following are examples of the language that different school mission statements use to describe an emphasis on job preparation:

- ◆ Develop productive, employable citizens
- ◆ Develop students who are prepared for quality jobs
- ◆ Encourage arts-related careers and lifelong arts appreciation
- ◆ Graduate students who can easily integrate into our workforce as skilled, productive, contributing citizens

Response to External Indicators

A third aspect of vocational development found in school mission statements is related to "metrics" for demonstrating proficiency. The language of the business community tends to fit well within the context of the vocational theme, and tangible, external indicators (or metrics) related to performance are an important element of the business world. The mission statement of Nature Coast Technical High School in Brooksville, Florida, provides a prototypical example:

> Nature Coast Technical High School's mission is to equip students with skills in technology, problem solving, critical thinking and social interactions by developing an atmosphere of trust, high expectations and consistent support. Our success will be measured through student achievement of maximum potential; parental, community, and employer satisfaction with our students; and improvement on standardized tests such as the FCAT, ACT and SAT.
>
> —Nature Coast Technical High School
> Brooksville, Florida (Vocational School, p. 56)

Common expressions and excerpts from school mission statements describing responses to external pressures follow:

- ◆ Provide experiential learning opportunities that will enable students to function proficiently within the parameters of the workplace
- ◆ Our success will be measured by employer satisfaction with our students

**Schools referencing the Vocational Development
theme in their mission statements:**

Page #	School Name	School Type
67	Advanced Technologies Academy, NV	Magnet
93	Archmere Academy, DE	Parochial
78	Compass Charter School, ID	Charter
133	Devine HS, TX	Award Winning School
121	Echo Lake ES, WA	Apple Distinguished School
70	McFatter Technical HS, FL	Magnet
55	Mercy Vocational HS, PA	Vocational
57	North County Trade Tech School, CA	Vocational
58	Oakland Technical HS, CA	Vocational
59	Paul M. Hodgson Vocational Tech HS, DE	Vocational
60	Pierson Vocational HS, AZ	Vocational
61	Queens Vocational and Technical HS, NY	Vocational
62	Region 10 Vocational HS, ME	Vocational
141	Ridge HS, NJ	Award Winning School
63	Smith Vocational and Agricultural HS, MA	Vocational
146	Trion HS, GA	Award Winning School
73	Waterbury Arts Magnet School, CT	Magnet
128	Westside HS, NE	Apple Distinguished School

Spiritual Development

Students' spiritual development is a rarely occurring theme across the sample of schools included in this book. Although most examples of this theme are found in the context of the parochial schools, we have observed spiritual development themes across public and private schools. When including spiritual development in their mission statements, schools generally employ one of two approaches:

1. Development of Specific Values
2. Holistic Emphasis

Development of Specific Values

Unlike the broader ethical/moral values invoked within the emotional development theme, here, the focus of the school mission statement is the spiritual development theme involving a specific set of values typically associated with a particular religious tradition. The mission statement of Montgomery Catholic Preparatory High School in Alabama provides an example:

> Montgomery Catholic Preparatory School is an integral part of the Catholic Church's mission to proclaim the gospel of Jesus Christ. As an adult community, we share in the responsibility to prepare students for college and beyond while helping them grow to become persons of faith, virtue and wisdom.
> —Montgomery Catholic Preparatory High School
> Montgomery, Alabama (Parochial School, p. 98)

The following are examples of the language that different school mission statements use to describe specific values within the context of spiritual development:

- ◆ Provide students with an education enriched by the values of love, respect, and justice
- ◆ Help students understand that life as a Christian is a journey that must be rooted in God
- ◆ As a school community, we seek to live the gospel in word and action
- ◆ Through the process of nurturing the soul, we offer students an intimate relationship with God
- ◆ Help students to become persons of faith, virtue, and wisdom
- ◆ Promote a dedication to faith reflection

Holistic Emphasis

A second aspect of the spiritual development theme we have found in school mission statements relates to the holistic development of students. Spiritual development is often invoked as one element of a holistic approach to education. The mission statement of Lilla G. Frederick Pilot Middle School in

Dorchester, Massachusetts, provides an example of a public school with a holistic emphasis:

> To provide students in grades six through eight with a rigorous academic curriculum within a stimulating and nurturing environment. The school serves the whole child—mind, body and spirit—as well as families and the community in which the children reside. Inquiry, exploration, experience, connections and hands-on learning all facilitate and complement the core academic curricula and support the school's vision of developing life-long learners.
> —Lilla G. Frederick Pilot Middle School
> Dorchester, Massachusetts (Apple School of Distinction, p. 124)

Common expressions and excerpts from school mission statements describing a holistic emphasis follow:

- Create an atmosphere for academic, emotional, and spiritual growth
- Awaken students and faculty to an inquiry into the meaning of their spiritual lives through religious studies, shared worship, campus ministry, and Christian service
- Understand students as beings of body, soul, and spirit and guide them to develop compassion and reverence for themselves and the world community
- Foster the harmonious development of spiritual, religious, intellectual, physical, emotional, and aesthetic gifts
- Provide our students with an education that enriches their spiritual and cultural development in order to develop the whole person
- We place the highest priority on the spiritual and moral development of our students and their service to others

Schools referencing the Spiritual Development theme in their mission statements:

Page #	School Name	School Type
93	Archmere Academy, DE	Parochial
108	The Bay School, ME	Waldorf
94	Brophy College Prep, AZ	Parochial
106	Emerson Waldorf School, NC	Waldorf
96	Father Gabriel Richard Catholic HS, MI	Parochial
97	Jesuit HS, OR	Parochial

Page #	School Name	School Type
124	Lilla G. Frederick Pilot Middle School, MA	Apple Distinguished School
55	Mercy Vocational HS, PA	Vocational
116	Montessori School at Holy Rosary, OH	Montessori
98	Montgomery Catholic Prep, AL	Parochial
90	Nuweetooun School, RI	Native American
99	Servite HS, CA	Parochial
100	St. Mary's HS, MO	Parochial

Physical Development

Consistent with findings from our past research, physical development was the least frequently cited theme in American school mission statements found across the sample of schools in this book. Typically, physical development is included in a school's mission statement as one of many components of a well-rounded education. Nay Ah Shing School in Onamia, Minnesota, provides a fairly typical example of how physical development is included in a school's mission statement, when it is included:

> The mission of Nay Ah Shing School is to teach Ojibwe Language, Culture, Tradition, History, and Skills to live in 2 cultures by:
>
> ◆ Educating students academically, socially, emotionally, and physically in a safe and supportive environment.
> ◆ Building relationships and socializing skills by teaching respect for themselves, for Elders and for all individuals.
> ◆ Creating strong partnerships with parents.
> ◆ Accomodation of learning styles and teaching life skills.
>
> —Nay Ah Shing School
> Onamia, Minnesota (Native American/Tribal School, p. 89)

The following are examples of the language that different school mission statements use to describe the importance of physical development:

◆ Understand the physical needs of students
◆ Support each child in his or her physical development
◆ Foster students academic, spiritual, and physical development
◆ Develop the whole person including the physical

- ◆ Serve the whole child—mind, body, spirit
- ◆ Ours is a place where strong bodies are nurtured

Schools referencing the Physical Development theme in their mission statements:

Page #	School Name	School Type
108	The Bay School, ME	Waldorf
115	Dynamite Montessori, AZ	Montessori
96	Father Gabriel Richard Catholic HS, MI	Parochial
33	Henry J. McLaughlin Jr. Middle School, NH	Public Middle School
107	Honolulu Waldorf School, HI	Waldorf
97	Jesuit HS, OR	Parochial
80	Jumoke Academy Charter School, CT	Charter
124	Lilla G. Frederick Pilot Middle School, MA	Apple Distinguished School
89	Nay Ah Shing School, MN	Native American
49	Rutland Senior High School, VT	Public High School

Conclusion

Many of today's most controversial and widely debated educational questions reflect, at their root, a basic lack of agreement about the underlying role and purpose of school. We hope this book demonstrates how mission statements can provide schools with an important opportunity to both define and communicate their fundamental purpose and role. The variety of school mission statements presented in this book highlight the broad range of goals that US schools pursue.

In the future, we believe that schools themselves could play a greater role in educational policy debate. For example, the current accountability movement associated with *No Child Left Behind* has been singularly focused on the cognitive domain. In fact, many public schools across the nation may face sanctions or even closure based almost entirely on state level standardized test scores in English Language Arts and Mathematics. Although we agree that schools should focus on cognitive skill development, this is only one of many important purposes purported by the majority of American public schools.

We feel that schools should be held accountable; however, current policies that use only one indicator to measure schools' success do a great disservice to the many American schools that espouse and articulate broader goals and purposes. Rather, schools should be accountable for those things that they themselves articulate as most important. In the past decade, we have witnessed how the heavy emphasis on cognitive outcomes has resulted in the neglect of the other important roles schools serve, both in practice as well as policy. The current accountability system is like evaluating the effectiveness of basketball players exclusively by how high they can jump: Although jumping is an important, if not critical, component to a basketball player's success, it fails to represent all of the other important components that make for a great teammate, strategist, etc.

If you are a school leader, we encourage you to view your mission statement as tool for defining those elements that are most highly valued in your local context. Once school goals are articulated and accepted in their mission statements, schools can begin discussions in their communities about how to demonstrate success across the full range of goals. For example, if your school emphasizes emotional development, clearly state that within your school mission and then think about ways you can show how the school is effectively fostering emotional development.

To continue the conversation about the purpose of school in America, to get more ideas on examining and constructing school mission statements, or to share your mission statement with us, please visit our website: http://www.purposeofschool.com.

Index of Schools by Grade Level

Schools Serving Students in Grades PreK-5

Page #	School Name	School Type
65	A.B. Combs Elementary, NC	Magnet School
76	Academy for Business and Leadership, FL	Charter School
112	Austin Montessori School, TX	Montessori
130	BASIS, AZ	Award Winning School
108	The Bay School, ME	Waldorf
68	Carter Academy, TX	Magnet School
114	Chesterfield Montessori School, MO	Montessori
86	Chief Leschi School, WA	Native American/Tribal
118	The Cobb School Montessori, CT	Montessori
77	Community Roots Charter School, NY	Charter School
78	Compass Charter School, ID	Charter School
104	Desert Marigold School, AZ	Waldorf
22	DeSoto Central Elementary School, MS	Public Elementary School
23	Dona Anna Elementary School, NM	Public Elementary School
115	Dynamite Montessori, AZ	Montessori
121	Echo Lake ES, WA	Apple
106	Emerson Waldorf School, NC	Waldorf
69	Forest Lake Elementary School, SC	Magnet School
87	Gila Crossing Community School, AZ	Native American/Tribal
24	Holiday Elementary School, KY	Public Elementary School
107	Honolulu Waldorf School, HI	Waldorf
123	Howard Elementary School, OR	Apple
25	Jerome Stamply Elementary School, MS	Public Elementary School
80	Jumoke Academy Charter School, CT	Charter School
81	KIPP Academy of Opportunity, CA	Charter School
82	KIPP Sunshine Peak Academy, CO	Charter School
26	Lincoln Elementary School, NM	Public Elementary School
116	Montessori School at Holy Rosary, OH	Montessori

Page #	School Name	School Type
98	Montgomery Catholic Prep, AL	Parochial
89	Nay Ah Shing School, MN	Native American/Tribal
71	Normal Park Museum Magnet, TN	Magnet School
90	Nuweetooun School, RI	Native American/Tribal
117	Pacific Rim International School, CA	Montessori
27	Parkside Elementary, WY	Public Elementary School
28	Providence Elementary School, UT	Public Elementary School
72	Richard J. Kinsella Magnet School of Performing Arts, CT	Magnet School
83	Rilke Schule German School of Arts & Sciences, AK	Charter School
29	Tombaugh Elementary School, NM	Public Elementary School
39	Tremont Middle School, IL	Public Middle School
109	Waldorf School of Princeton, NJ	Waldorf
110	Waldorf School on the Roaring Fork, CO	Waldorf

Schools Serving Students in Grades 6-8

Page #	School Name	School Type
76	Academy for Business and Leadership, FL	Charter School
112	Austin Montessori School, TX	Montessori
130	BASIS, AZ	Award Winning School
108	The Bay School, ME	Waldorf
31	Beresford Middle School, SD	Public Middle School
95	Cardinal Newman School, SC	Parochial
114	Chesterfield Montessori School, MO	Montessori
86	Chief Leschi School, WA	Native American/Tribal
118	The Cobb School Montessori, CT	Montessori
78	Compass Charter School, ID	Charter School
120	Del Mar Middle School, CA	Apple
104	Desert Marigold School, AZ	Waldorf
35	Dr. Martin Luther King, Jr. Middle School, MD	Public Middle School
121	Echo Lake ES, WA	Apple
106	Emerson Waldorf School, NC	Waldorf

Page #	School Name	School Type
87	Gila Crossing Community School, AZ	Native American/Tribal
32	Glen Crest Middle School, IL	Public Middle School
33	Henry J. McLaughlin Middle School, NH	Public Middle School
107	Honolulu Waldorf School, HI	Waldorf
80	Jumoke Academy Charter School, CT	Charter School
88	Kayenta Middle School, AZ	Native American/Tribal
34	Kingsley Junior High School, IL	Public Middle School
81	KIPP Academy of Opportunity, CA	Charter School
82	KIPP Sunshine Peak Academy, CO	Charter School
137	Leo Junior/Senior HS, IN	Award Winning School
124	Lilla G. Frederick Middle School, MA	Apple
116	Montessori School at Holy Rosary, OH	Montessori
98	Montgomery Catholic Prep, AL	Parochial
89	Nay Ah Shing School, MN	Native American/Tribal
71	Normal Park Museum Magnet, TN	Magnet School
90	Nuweetooun School, RI	Native American/Tribal
59	Paul M. Hodgson Vocational Tech HS, DE	Vocational/Career/ Technical Education
139	Preuss UCSD, CA	Award Winning School
36	Princeton Middle School, WV	Public Middle School
72	Richard J. Kinsella Magnet School of Performing Arts, CT	Magnet School
83	Rilke Schule German School of Arts & Sciences, AK	Charter School
142	Rock Creek Junior/Senior HS, KS	Award Winning School
37	Sioux Valley Middle School, SD	Public Middle School
38	Timberlane Middle School, NH	Public Middle School
39	Tremont Middle School, IL	Public Middle School
109	Waldorf School of Princeton, NJ	Waldorf
110	Waldorf School on the Roaring Fork, CO	Waldorf
127	Washington Middle School, WI	Apple
73	Waterbury Arts Magnet School, CT	Magnet School
40	Westwood Middle School, WV	Public Middle School
41	Windham Middle School, NH	Public Middle School

Schools Serving Students in Grades 9-12

Page #	School Name	School Type
103	Academe of the Oaks, GA	Waldorf
66	Academic Magnet HS, SC	Magnet School
67	Advanced Technologies Academy, NV	Magnet School
93	Archmere Academy, DE	Parochial
130	BASIS, AZ	Award Winning School
44	Bellows Free Academy, VT	Public High School
43	Bentonville High School, AR	Public High School
45	Billings West High School, MT	Public High School
149	Bodine HS for International Affairs, PA	Award Winning School
46	Bossier High School, LA	Public High School
94	Brophy College Prep, AZ	Parochial
95	Cardinal Newman School, SC	Parochial
131	Chapin HS, SC	Award Winning School
86	Chief Leschi School, WA	Native American/Tribal
132	Columbiana HS, OH	Award Winning School
78	Compass Charter School, ID	Charter School
104	Desert Marigold School, AZ	Waldorf
133	Devine HS, TX	Award Winning School
134	Eastside HS, FL	Award Winning School
106	Emerson Waldorf School, NC	Waldorf
122	Empire HS, AZ	Apple
96	Father Gabriel Richard Catholic HS, MI	Parochial
79	Harding Fine Arts Academy, OK	Charter School
47	Hellgate High School, MT	Public High School
135	Hingham High School, MA	Award Winning School
107	Honolulu Waldorf School, HI	Waldorf
97	Jesuit HS, OR	Parochial
136	Lakeville North HS, MN	Award Winning School
137	Leo Junior/Senior HS, IN	Award Winning School
70	McFatter Technical HS, FL	Magnet School
55	Mercy Vocational HS, PA	Vocational/Career/ Technical Education
138	Middle College HS, CA	Award Winning School

Page #	School Name	School Type
98	Montgomery Catholic Prep, AL	Parochial
48	Montpelier High School, VT	Public High School
56	Nature Coast Technical HS, FL	Vocational/Career/ Technical Education
89	Nay Ah Shing School, MN	Native American/Tribal
57	North County Trade Tech School, CA	Vocational/Career/ Technical Education
58	Oakland Technical HS, CA	Vocational/Career/ Technical Education
59	Paul M. Hodgson Vocational Tech HS, DE	Vocational/Career/ Technical Education
60	Pierson Vocational HS, AZ	Vocational/Career/ Technical Education
139	Preuss UCSD, CA	Award Winning School
61	Queens Vocational and Technical HS, NY	Vocational/Career/ Technical Education
62	Region 10 Vocational HS, ME	Vocational/Career/ Technical Education
141	Ridge HS, NJ	Award Winning School
142	Rock Creek Junior/Senior HS, KS	Award Winning School
49	Rutland Senior High School, VT	Public High School
143	School of Science and Engineering, TX	Award Winning School
144	School for the Talented and Gifted, TX	Award Winning School
125	Science Leadership Academy, PA	Apple
99	Servite HS, CA	Parochial
63	Smith Vocational and Agricultural HS, MA	Vocational/Career/ Technical Education
50	South High School, ND	Public High School
100	St. Mary's HS, MO	Parochial
145	Thomas Jefferson High School for Science and Technology, VA	Award Winning School
101	Totino-Grace HS, MN	Parochial
146	Trion HS, GA	Award Winning School
126	The Urban School of San Francisco, CA	Apple
147	Vestavia HS, AL	Award Winning School
73	Waterbury Arts Magnet School, CT	Magnet School
148	West Lyon HS, IA	Award Winning School

Page #	School Name	School Type
128	Westside HS, NE	Apple
51	Winooski High School, VT	Public High School
52	Wynne High School, AR	Public High School

Index of Schools by Urbanicity

City

Page #	School Name	School Type
65	A.B. Combs Elementary, NC	Magnet School
66	Academic Magnet HS, SC	Magnet School
67	Advanced Techologies Academy, NV	Magnet School
112	Austin Montessori School, TX	Montessori
130	BASIS, AZ	Award Winning School
43	Bentonville High School, AR	Public High School
45	Billings West High School, MT	Public High School
149	Bodine HS for International Affairs, PA	Award Winning School
46	Bossier High School, LA	Public High School
94	Brophy College Prep, AZ	Parochial
113	Casa Dei Bambini, GA	Montessori
77	Community Roots Charter School, NY	Charter School
104	Desert Marigold School, AZ	Waldorf
79	Harding Fine Arts Academy, OK	Charter School
47	Hellgate High School, MT	Public High School
33	Henry J. McLaughlin Middle School, NH	Public Middle School
107	Honolulu Waldorf School, HI	Waldorf
123	Howard Elementary School, OR	Apple
97	Jesuit HS, OR	Parochial
80	Jumoke Academy Charter School, CT	Charter School
34	Kingsley Junior High School, IL	Public Middle School
81	KIPP Academy of Opportunity, CA	Charter School
82	KIPP Sunshine Peak Academy, CO	Charter School
124	Lilla G. Frederick Middle School, MA	Apple
55	Mercy Vocational HS, PA	Vocational
138	Middle College HS, CA	Award Winning School
116	Montessori School at Holy Rosary, OH	Montessori
98	Montgomery Catholic Prep, AL	Parochial
71	Normal Park Museum Magnet, TN	Magnet School

Page #	School Name	School Type
58	Oakland Technical HS, CA	Vocational
139	Preuss UCSD, CA	Award Winning School
61	Queens Vocational and Technical HS, NY	Vocational
72	Richard J. Kinsella Magnet School of Performing Arts, CT	Magnet School
83	Rilke Schule German School of Arts & Sciences, AK	Charter School
144	School for the Talented and Gifted, TX	Award Winning School
143	School of Science and Engineering, TX	Award Winning School
125	Science Leadership Academy, PA	Apple
99	Servite HS, CA	Parochial
50	South High School, ND	Public High School
100	St. Mary's HS, MO	Parochial
126	The Urban School of San Francisco, CA	Apple
128	Westside HS, NE	Apple

Suburb

Page #	School Name	School Type
103	Academe of the Oaks, GA	Waldorf
76	Academy for Business and Leadership, FL	Charter School
93	Archmere Academy, DE	Parochial
108	The Bay School, ME	Waldorf
95	Cardinal Newman School, SC	Parochial
68	Carter Academy, TX	Magnet School
114	Chesterfield Montessori School, MO	Montessori
118	The Cobb School Montessori, CT	Montessori
78	Compass Charter School, ID	Charter School
120	Del Mar Middle School, CA	Apple
23	Doña Anna Elementary School, NM	Public Elementary School
35	Dr. Martin Luther King, Jr. Middle School, MD	Public Middle School
115	Dynamite Montessori, AZ	Montessori
134	Eastside HS, FL	Award Winning School
121	Echo Lake ES, WA	Apple
69	Forest Lake Elementary School, SC	Magnet School
32	Glen Crest Middle School, IL	Public Middle School
135	Hingham High School, MA	Award Winning School

Page #	School Name	School Type
136	Lakeville North HS, MN	Award Winning School
137	Leo Junior/Senior HS, IN	Award Winning School
70	McFatter Technical HS, FL	Magnet School
56	Nature Coast Technical HS, FL	Vocational
117	Pacific Rim International School, CA	Montessori
59	Paul M. Hodgson Vocational Tech HS, DE	Vocational
28	Providence Elementary School, UT	Public Elementary School
141	Ridge HS, NJ	Award Winning School
63	Smith Vocational and Agricultural HS, MA	Vocational
145	Thomas Jefferson High School for Science and Technology, VA	Award Winning School
38	Timberlane Middle School, NH	Public Middle School
29	Tombaugh Elementary School, NM	Public Elementary School
101	Totino-Grace HS, MN	Parochial
147	Vestavia HS, AL	Award Winning School
109	Waldorf School of Princeton, NJ	Waldorf
127	Washington Middle School, WI	Apple
73	Waterbury Arts Magnet School, CT	Magnet School
51	Winooski High School, VT	Public High School

Town

Page #	School Name	School Type
132	Columbiana HS, OH	Award Winning School
133	Devine HS, TX	Award Winning School
24	Holiday Elementary School, KY	Public Elementary School
25	Jerome Stamply Elementary School, MS	Public Elementary School
26	Lincoln Elementary School, NM	Public Elementary School
48	Montpelier High School, VT	Public High School
27	Parkside Elementary, WY	Public Elementary School
60	Pierson Vocational HS, AZ	Vocational
36	Princeton Middle School, WV	Public Middle School
49	Rutland Senior High School, VT	Public High School
146	Trion HS, GA	Award Winning School
52	Wynne High School, AR	Public High School

Rural

Page #	School Name	School Type
44	Bellows Free Academy, VT	Public High School
31	Beresford Middle School, SD	Public Middle School
131	Chapin HS, SC	Award Winning School
22	DeSoto Central Elementary School, MS	Public Elementary School
106	Emerson Waldorf School, NC	Waldorf
122	Empire HS, AZ	Apple
96	Father Gabriel Richard Catholic HS, MI	Parochial
88	Kayenta Middle School, AZ	Native American
57	North County Trade Tech School, CA	Vocational
90	Nuweetooun School, RI	Native American
62	Region 10 Vocational HS, ME	Vocational
142	Rock Creek Junior/Senior HS, KS	Award Winning School
37	Sioux Valley Middle School, SD	Public Middle School
39	Tremont Middle School, IL	Public Middle School
110	Waldorf School on the Roaring Fork, CO	Waldorf
148	West Lyon HS, IA	Award Winning School
40	Westwood Middle School, WV	Public Middle School
41	Windham Middle School, NH	Public Middle School

Unclassified

Page #	School Name	School Type
86	Chief Leschi School, WA	Native American
87	Gila Crossing Community School, AZ	Native American
89	Nay Ah Shing School, MN	Native American

Index of Schools by Percent of Students Eligible for Free or Reduced-Price Lunch

Page #	School Name	Percent	School Type
139	Preuss UCSD, CA	99.6	Award Winning School
72	Richard J. Kinsella Magnet School of Performing Arts, CT	99.5	Magnet School
25	Jerome Stamply Elementary School, MS	97	Public Elementary School
82	KIPP Sunshine Peak Academy, CO	93.3	Charter School
60	Pierson Vocational HS, AZ	91	Vocational
88	Kayenta Middle School, AZ	90.6	Native American
68	Carter Academy, TX	86.2	Magnet School
124	Lilla G. Frederick Middle School, MA	85.9	Apple
81	KIPP Academy of Opportunity, CA	85.6	Charter School
26	Lincoln Elementary School, NM	85	Public Elementary School
23	Doña Anna Elementary School, NM	75.4	Public Elementary School
61	Queens Vocational and Technical HS, NY	73.2	Vocational
51	Winooski High School, VT	71.5	Public High School
123	Howard Elementary School, OR	69.8	Apple
46	Bossier High School, LA	67.8	Public High School
138	Middle College HS, CA	66.6	Award Winning School
29	Tombaugh Elementary School, NM	64.8	Public Elementary School
24	Holiday Elementary School, KY	60.3	Public Elementary School
127	Washington Middle School, WI	60.1	Apple
40	Westwood Middle School, WV	58.1	Public Middle School
79	Harding Fine Arts Academy, OK	56.4	Charter School
58	Oakland Technical HS, CA	56.4	Vocational
143	School of Science and Engineering, TX	54.9	Award Winning School
69	Forest Lake Elementary School, SC	52.7	Magnet School
36	Princeton Middle School, WV	51.3	Public Middle School
57	North County Trade Tech School, CA	51.2	Vocational
73	Waterbury Arts Magnet School, CT	50.4	Magnet School
52	Wynne High School, AR	49.7	Public High School
80	Jumoke Academy Charter School, CT	48.6	Charter School

Page #	School Name	Percent	School Type
27	Parkside Elementary, WY	47.1	Public Elementary School
33	Henry J. McLaughlin Middle School, NH	45.6	Public Middle School
149	Bodine HS for International Affairs, PA	43.6	Award Winning School
134	Eastside HS, FL	41.7	Award Winning School
133	Devine HS, TX	39.2	Award Winning School
35	Dr. Martin Luther King, Jr. Middle School, MD	39	Public Middle School
132	Columbiana HS, OH	36.1	Award Winning School
56	Nature Coast Technical HS, FL	36	Vocational
77	Community Roots Charter School, NY	35.1	Charter School
121	Echo Lake ES, WA	33.7	Apple
47	Hellgate High School, MT	33.2	Public High School
63	Smith Vocationaland Agricultural HS, MA	33	Vocational
49	Rutland Senior High School, VT	31.7	Public High School
144	School for the Talented and Gifted, TX	27.5	Award Winning School
78	Compass Charter School, ID	27.3	Charter School
34	Kingsley Junior High School, IL	27	Public Middle School
142	Rock Creek Junior/Senior HS, KS	26.5	Award Winning School
31	Beresford Middle School, SD	25.1	Public Middle School
70	McFatter Technical HS, FL	25	Magnet School
148	West Lyon HS, IA	24.4	Award Winning School
22	DeSoto Central Elementary School, MS	23.8	Public Elementary School
43	Bentonville High School, AR	23.4	Public High School
28	Providence Elementary School, UT	23.3	Public Elementary School
125	Science Leadership Academy, PA	22.4	Apple
71	Normal Park Museum Magnet, TN	21	Magnet School
50	South High School, ND	19.6	Public High School
37	Sioux Valley Middle School, SD	19.5	Public Middle School
48	Montpelier High School, VT	19.2	Public High School
67	Advanced Techologies Academy, NV	19.1	Magnet School
44	Bellows Free Academy, VT	17.9	Public High School
146	Trion HS, GA	17.5	Award Winning School
59	Paul M. Hodgson Vocational Tech HS, DE	17.3	Vocational
45	Billings West High School, MT	16.8	Public High School
128	Westside HS, NE	16.5	Apple

Page #	School Name	Percent	School Type
38	Timberlane Middle School, NH	14.6	Public Middle School
104	Desert Marigold School, AZ	14.1	Waldorf
122	Empire HS, AZ	11.9	Apple
39	Tremont Middle School, IL	9.6	Public Middle School
131	Chapin HS, SC	9.5	Award Winning School
137	Leo Junior/Senior HS, IN	8.9	Award Winning School
66	Academic Magnet HS, SC	6.5	Magnet School
41	Windham Middle School, NH	5.7	Public Middle School
136	Lakeville North HS, MN	5	Award Winning School
147	Vestavia HS, AL	4.5	Award Winning School
135	Hingham High School, MA	3.1	Award Winning School
145	Thomas Jefferson High School for Science and Technology, VA	1.3	Award Winning School
141	Ridge HS, NJ	0.7	Award Winning School

References

187th General Court of the Commonwealth of Massachusetts. (2010). *Constitution of the Commonwealth of Massachusetts*. Retrieved from http://www.state.ma.us/legis/const.htm

Abrahams, J. (2007). *101 Mission Statements from Top Companies*. Berkeley, CA: Ten Speed Press.

Adler, M. J. (1982). *The Paidea proposal: An educational manifesto*. New York: Collier Macmillan.

AdvancED. (2010). *Accreditation standards, indicators, and impact statements for quality schools*. Accessed August 31, 2010 at: http://www.advanc-ed.org/webfm_send/10.

Association for Career and Technical Education. (2011). *About ACTE*. Retrieved from http://www.acteonline.org/about.aspx.

Association of Waldorf Schools of North America. (n.d.). *Why Waldorf works*. Retrieved from http://www.whywaldorfworks.org/.

Bebell, D., & Kay, R. (2010, Jan.). One to one computing: A summary of the quantitative results from the Berkshire Wireless Learning Initiative. *The Journal of Technology, Learning and Assessment*. Retrieved from http://escholarship.bc.edu/jtla/vol9/2/.

Bebell, D., & Stemler, S. E. (2004, April). *Reassessing the objectives of educational accountability in Massachusetts: The mismatch between Massachusetts and the MCAS*. Paper presented at the American Educational Research Association, San Diego, CA.

Berleur, J., & Harvanek, R. F. (1997). *Analysis of mission statements or similar documents of Jesuit universities and higher education institutions*. Retrieved October 17, 2002, from http://www.info.fundp.ac.be/~jbl/mis-stat/index.htm

Center for Education Reform. (2011). Retrieved July 10, 2011, from http://www.edreform.com/Issues/Charter_Connection/.

Center for Research on Educational Outcomes. (2009). *Multiple-choice: Charter school performance in 16 states*. Stanford, California: Stanford University.

Chen, G. (2007). What is a magnet school? *Public School Review*. Retrieved from http://www.publicschoolreview.com/articles/2.

Claus, R. N., & Chamaine, J. (1985, October). *An assessment of the Saginaw successful schools project: A look at the data*. Paper presented at the Joint meeting of the Evaluation Research Society and the Evaluation Network, Toronto, Canada.

Colmant, S.A. (2000). U.S. and Canadian boarding schools: A review, past and present. *Native Americas Journal 17*(4), 24–30.

Counts, G. S. (1978). *Dare the schools build a new social order?* Carbondale, IL: Southern Illinois University Press.

The Daily Beast. (2010). *From Newsweek: America's best high schools 2010*. Retrieved from http://www.newsweek.com/feature/2010/americas-best-high-schools.html.

deMarrais, K. B., & LeCompte, M. D. (1995). *The way schools work: A sociological analysis of education (2nd ed.)*. White Plains, NY: Longman Publishers.

Dewey, J. (1938). *Experience and education*. New York: Simon and Schuster.

Dohrmann, K. R., Nishida, T., Gartner, A., Lipsky, D., & Grimm, K. (2007). High school outcomes for students in a public Montessori program. *Journal of Research in Childhood Education, 22*, 205–217. doi: 10.1080/02568540709594622.

Druian, G., & Butler, J. A. B. (1987). *Effective schooling practices and at-risk youth: What the research shows*. Portland, OR: Northwest Regional Educational Laboratory.

Emil, A. (2001). *The Fieldstone Alliance Guide to Crafting Effective Mission and Vision Statements*. Saint Paul, MN: Wilder.

Florida Legislature. (2010). *The Florida constitution*. Retrieved from http://www.leg.state.fl.us/Statutes/index.cfm?Mode=Constitution&Submenu=3&Tab=statutes#A09

Gardner, P.D. (2007). *Recruiting Trends: 2006-2007*. East Lansing, MI: Collegiate Employment Research Institute, Michigan State University.

Goodlad, J.I. (1979). *What schools are for*. Bloomington, IN: Phi Delta Kappa Educational Foundation.

Hammerschlag, C., Alderfer, C. P., & Berg, D. (1973). Indian education: A human systems analysis. *American Journal of Psychiatry 130*(10), 1098–1102.

Immerwahl, J. (2000). *Great expectations: How Californians view higher education*. San Jose, CA: National Center for Public Policy and Higher Education and Public Agenda.

John J. Heldrich Center for Workforce Development. (2005). *Survey of New Jersey employers to assess the ability of higher education institutions to prepare students for employment*. Newark, NJ: Rutgers, The state university of New Jersey.

Knight, G.R. (1989). *Issues and Alternatives in Educational Philosophy (2nd Ed.)*. Berrien Springs, Michigan: Andrews University Press.

Labaree, D. F. (1997). *How to succeed in school without really learning*. New Haven, CT: Yale University Press.

Levesque, K., Laird, J., Hensley, E., Choy, S. P., Cataldi, E. F., & Hudson, L. (2008). *Career and technical education in the United States: 1990 to 2005 (NCES 2008–035)*. Washington, DC: National Center for Education Statistics, Institute of Education Sciences, US Department of Education.

Magnet Schools of America. (2007). *Who we are*. Retrieved from http://www.magnet.edu/modules/info/who_we_are.html.

McDonald, D., & Schultz, M. (2009).*United States Catholic elementary and secondary schools 2009–2010 annual statistical report on schools, enrollment and staffing*. Arlington, VA: National Catholic Education Association.

McDuffy v. Secretary, 1993, 415 Mass. 545.

Montessori Foundation. (2011). *Welcome to the Montessori Foundation*. Retrieved from http://www.montessori.org/.

National Catholic Education Association. (2010a). *A brief overview of Catholic schools in America*. Retrieved from http://www.ncea.org/about/HistoricalOverviewofCatholicSchoolsInAmerica.asp.

National Catholic Education Association. (2010b). *Catholic school data*. Retrieved from http://www.ncea.org/news/AnnualDataReport.asp.

National Charter School Resource Center. (n.d.). Retrieved July 10, 2011, from http://www.uscharterschools.org/pub/uscs_docs/o/index.htm.

Noddings, N. (1995). *Philosophy of education*. Boulder, CO: Westview Press.

Perkins, D. (1992). *Smart schools: Better thinking and learning for every child*. New York, NY: Free Press.

Reed, R. F., & Johnson, T. W. (Eds.). (1996). *Philosophical documents in education*. White Plains, NY: Longman Publishers, Inc.

Renchler, R. (1991). Leadership with a vision: How principals develop and implement their visions for school success. *OSSC Bulletin, 34*(5), 1-29.

Renihan, P. J., Renihan, F. I., & Waldron, P. (1986). The common ingredients of successful school effectiveness projects. *Education Canada, 26*(3), 16-21.

Rose v. Council for Better Education, 790 S.W. 2d 186 (1989).

Rutter, M., & Maughan, B. (2002). School effectiveness findings 1979-2002. *Journal of school psychology, 40*(6), 451-475.

RWM.org: Vocational Schools Database. (2011). *Find vocational schools by clicking on a state*. Retrieved from http://www.rwm.org/rwm/.

Schiro, M. (1978). *Curriculum for better schools*. Englewood Cliffs, NJ: Educational Technology Publications, Inc.

Stemler, S. E. (2001). An overview of content analysis. *Practical Assessment, Research and Evaluation, 7*(17), Available online: http://ericae.net/pare/getvn.asp?v=7&n=17.

Stemler, S. E., & Bebell, D. (April, 1999). *An empirical approach to understanding and analyzing the mission statements of selected educational institutions*. Paper presented at the New England Educational Research Organization (NEERO), Portsmouth, NH.

Stemler, S. E., & Bebell, D., & Sonnabend, L. (2011). Using school mission statements for reflection and research. *Educational Administration Quarterly, 47*(2), 383-420.

Stober, S. S. (1997). *A content analysis of college and university mission statements. Unpublished doctoral dissertation*, Temple University, Philadelphia, PA.

Tanner, D., & Tanner, L. (1990). *History of the school curriculum*. New York: Macmillan Publishing Company.

Teddlie, C., & Reynolds, D. (Eds.). (2000). *The international handbook of school effectiveness research*. New York: Falmer Press.

TribalBiz.com. (n.d.). *Native American K–12 resources*. Retrieved from http://www.tribalbiz.com/native_american_k-12_resources.php.

Tyack, D. B. (1988). Ways of seeing: An essay on the history of compulsory schooling. In R. M. Jaeger (Ed.), *Complementary methods for research in education (pp. 24-59)*. Washington, DC: American Educational Research Association.

US Conference of Catholic Bishops (USCCB). (2008). *Doctrinal Elements of a curriculum framework for the development of catechetical materials for young people of high school age*. Retrieved from http://www.usccb.org/about/evangelization-and-catechesis/catechesis/upload/high-school-curriculum-framework-adaptation-of-preamble-2.pdf.

US Department of Education. (2011a). *National Blue Ribbon Schools Program*. Retrieved from http://www2.ed.gov/programs/nclbbrs/index.html.

US Department of Education. (2011b). *Office of vocational and adult education*. Retrieved from http://www2.ed.gov/about/offices/list/ovae/index.html.

US Department of Education, National Center for Education Statistics. (n.d.). *Digest of educational statistics*: *Age range for compulsory school attendance and special education services, and policies on year-round schools and kindergarten programs,*

by state: Selected years, 1997 through 2008. Retrieved from http://nces.ed.gov/
programs/digest/d08/tables/dt08_165.asp.

US Department of Education, National Center for Education Statistics (2008). Career
and Technical Education in the United States: 1990-2005 (NCES 2008–035).

US Department of Education, National Center for Education Statistics. (2010). *Statistics of state school systems, 1967–68 and 1975–76; Statistics of public elementary and
secondary day schools, 1970–71, 1972–73, 1974–75, and 1976–77 through 1980–81;
and Common core of data (CCD), "Public Elementary/Secondary School Universe
Survey," 1982–83 through 2008–09.*

US Department of Education, National Center for Education Statistics. (2011).
Digest of Education Statistics, 2010 (NCES 2011–015), Table 5. Retrieved from
http://nces.ed.gov/programs/digest/d08/tables/dt08_165.asp.

US News. (2009). *Best high schools: State-by-state statistics.* Retrieved from http://
education.usnews.rankingsandreviews.com/education/high-schools/
articles/2009/12/09/americas-best-high-schools-state-by-state-statistics.

Waldorf School Association. (n.d.) Retrieved from http://www.waldorfschule.info.

Wikipedia Foundation. (2007). *Americanization of Native Americans.* Retrieved from
http://en.wikipedia.org/wiki/Americanization_of_Native_Americans.

Word List of Rudolf Steiner (Waldorf) Schools and Teacher Training Centers. (2011).
Retrieved from http://waldorfschule.info/upload/pdf/schulliste.pdf.

Yeboah, A. (2005). *Education among Native Americans in the periods before and after contact with Europeans: An overview.* Paper presented at the National Association of
Native American Studies Conference, February 14 to 19, 2005, Houston, Texas.